Filling the Void:

A Selection of Humanist and Atheist Poetry

Edited by
Jonathan MS Pearce

Foreword by Andrew Copson

Afterword by Dale McGowan

Filling the Void: A Selection of Humanist and Atheist Poetry

Trade paperback ISBN: 978-0-9926000-8-2

OB 11/17

Praise for this volume:

"In Filling the Void, Jonathan MS Pearce has put together an anthology of valuable literature for humanity. Verse speaks to us in ways that prose cannot, and here, for those lacking belief in God, we find people given an often-silent voice. Sometimes wry, sometimes struggling, sometimes defiant, poignant, or beautiful, the poetry in *Filling the Void* expresses the contemporary nonbeliever's experience in truly human terms."

James A. Lindsay,
author of *Dot, Dot, Dot: Infinity Plus God Equals Folly*
and *Everybody Is Wrong About God*

"Read this extraordinary book;
feel the wonder and take delight in the fact that
we are that singular facet of the universe
able to contemplate itself
through science and art
and to create poetry
in the intersection
of the two."

David Fitzgerald,
author of *Nailed* and
The Complete Heretic's Guide to Western Religion series

"Divinity Pearced by worded structure
Wandering from blinding sands to southern birds
Poems for our secular times

This anthology of freethinking poems, ranging from poignant to humorous, from ancient voices to modern songs, encapsulates the thoughts of many secular folks. See what a few meters of these works may do for you and inspire further reflection in a new way."

Dr. Aaron Adair,
author of *The Star of Bethlehem: A Skeptical View*

"Jonathan Pearce has done us a great service in producing this anthology. *Filling the Void* is eclectic, witty, arresting, philosophical, and fun. It charts a course through the emotional landscape of atheism and fills a niche in humanist literature that's been vacant for far too long."

David Warden,
Chair of Dorset Humanists

"Many books about atheism focus on science or challenging religious dogma so it can be difficult to find literature on how nonbelievers find meaning in their lives. *Filling the Void* shares the perspectives of a diverse group of atheists who express how they grapple with reality and their emotions. Jonathan Pearce has provided a necessary addition to atheist and humanist literature with this beautiful anthology."

Matthew Facciani,
sociologist and activist, blogger at *According to Matthew*

"This collection vibrantly showcases the fact that having a naturalistic, scientific worldview in no way means one can't experience the grandeur and majesty of life and the universe...or have a wickedly keen sense of humor about that whole god idea. *Filling the Void* should do just that for most readers: plug a hole in their book collection nicely, showcasing the overlap of humanism and literature, of science and verse, of religious criticism and rhyming constants."

Dr. Caleb Lack,
Director of the Secular Therapist Project; author of *Critical Thinking, Science, & Pseudoscience: Why We Can't Trust Our Brains*

I loved this book of poems, mainly for its huge variety of styles, subject matter and the very varied starting points of the authors. Whilst the title suggests that it is aimed at those currently seeking meaning, I found that there was much food for thought both for someone who is living happily without gods, and for the committed religious person who is interested in other points of view. This was down to the authenticity of the chosen authors. And like all books of poems, it's perfect for dipping into at will.

Clio Bellenis,
psychiatrist and Committee Member of The Hampshire Skeptics

*For those trying to break out from whatever
is unfairly constraining them.
May they have a voice.*

*And for Julian Haydon –
carrying Ingersoll's torch.*

Acknowledgements

This book would not have been possible without the contributors themselves, called from various places in various ways. I am also indebted to Andrew Copson for writing the foreword and to Dale McGowan for the afterword. As ever, Ed Babinski was a useful resource, and a generally good fellow for putting me on to many of the poets. Thanks to Shelley Segal for allowing her very great songs from her *Atheist Album* to be included within this anthology; I implore the readers to go out and buy her album—great music and lyrics about things that we all find fascinating. There is something fulfilling about cerebral music which flicks switches that more mainstream music just cannot do. Which brings me on to Steve and Tally Cass, whose poems here are slightly adapted from their lyrics for their rock band Monster on Sunday. Please check them out here http://monsteronsunday.com where you can find out everything about them. It seems there is a growing supply and demand for atheistic music. Thanks muchly to them for their poems/lyrics herein! I am very grateful to Rex Pay at Humanistic Texts (http://www.humanistictexts.org) who has provided translations for the Abul ʿAla Al-Maʿarri poems within the collection. Lastly, thanks to Kevin Friery for the lovely cover images and Jules Bailey for cover design assistance.

A Note on Styles

These poems come from different corners of the world. As such, the writing styles and protocol differs. Rather than normalise the styles to create a uniformity, I have decided to keep the source styles and conventions of the original writers. This is because poetry is often very personal, and changing spelling and other syntactical conventions can be a thorn in the side for some poets and writers. I hope the differences do not cause too much discomfort for the writer, and may even give hints to the provenance of the pieces.

About the Editor

Jonathan MS Pearce is a philosopher, author, blogger and teacher who lives in Fareham, Hampshire, UK with his partner and twin boys. He has spent many years philosophising about all things religious and...well, all things, actually. He has a penchant for discussing free will, or its illusion, and how this affects society. Pearce has written a number of books, edited others, and contributed to more still, and public speaks to various groups around the UK concerning the topics he covers. He is surprised there is any time left in the day to breathe. You can find him on the Patheos network, blogging at *A Tippling Philosopher* (patheos.com/blogs/tippling).

Other books by Jonathan MS Pearce include:

Free Will? An investigation into whether we have free will or whether I was always going to write this book

The Little Book Of Unholy Questions

The Nativity: A Critical Examination

Beyond An Absence of Faith: Stories About the Loss of Faith and the Discovery of Self (ed.)

The Problem With "God" (ebook)

13 Reasons To Doubt (ed.)

CONTENTS

Foreword

By Andrew Copson

Some people see the arts—whether the visual arts, music, the dramatic arts, or the arts of literature—as the icing on the cake of life, that little bit extra that helps to get us through. Nothing could be further from the truth. The arts—and literature in particular—are not an extra sweetener, but a vital part of a fully human life.

For me, verse is the epitome of this. It can express the most profound observations about the universe, this world, and ourselves in ways that are beautiful and uniquely evocative, in ways that stay with us. We remember a poem or a few lines of a poem in a way that we seldom remember a few lines of prose. As the words stay with us, the thoughts they express are continually reconsidered by us, subconsciously and consciously, and they change us.

Atheists, not in thrall to one book alone, are free to dip into all the books. Humanists, believing that there is one life and that we make whatever meaning and purpose it has for ourselves, enlist literature as part of that meaning-making process. Acknowledging the human species as one and human cultures all over the world as our common heritage, we see, rolling out before us, literature from a dazzling range of times and places, sentiments and standpoints.

As wide a possible engagement with as many thoughts, sentiments, stories, and poems as possible will help us become more thoughtful, more open-minded, and more human. As Bertrand Russell said (in a memorable bit of prose), "The secret of happiness is this: let your interest be as wide as possible and let your reactions to the things and persons who interest you be as far as possible friendly rather than hostile." I'm sure this advice holds good as we engage with the arts as much as those other things. May you find many new friends in this volume!

Andrew Copson
Chief Executive,
British Humanist Association

Introduction

By Jonathan MS Pearce

Atheism doesn't say much. Unless you think God is a major thing. In which case it says a bit more. The reality is, a lack of belief in God, or a positive belief that God doesn't exist, doesn't necessarily say much more about life, the universe and everything. That takes a bit more effort; that takes building your worldview up from scratch until you get something coherent and holistic; in short, that takes philosophy.

So without saying too much, atheism requires add-ons and plug-ins to convert it into a meaningful and pragmatic system with which to tackle life and all of the challenges it throws at you. Enter stage right humanism. As a non-religious answer to, well, religion, it is able to equip people with the tools to sculpt life and meaning out of mere matter. Humans have a remarkable capacity for humanity. It seems trivially true, but the point is quite underestimated. Humanity has its basis in humanity, in humankind. There is no need for God to account for and propagate meaning, morality, culture, art, creativity, abstracts and so on, in our lives. We can do that perfectly well on our own, thank you very much.

In fact, there is a sense that the act of defining our life's meaning, for example, is much nobler when defined by ourselves. We don't need to be lazy and adopt some deity's meaning and purpose for ourselves. It takes more work, granted, but when we sculpt meaning with our own tools, out of our own material, then there is something so much more gratifying when sitting back and inspecting and appreciating the end result. "I did that."

And when we come together harmoniously, as humankind, and work towards bettering ourselves and our world, using those

3

same tools, then we can all look back at the real and abstract edifices we have built up and smile. "We did that."

When humanity works, it's a beautiful thing. And this book goes some way to celebrate that. To celebrate the questioning mind, the critical mind, the scientific mind, the philosophical mind. And yes, there are some critical pieces herein. God does not get off lightly (it's okay, he can't mind: he's not there!). Religion does not get off lightly. There is a certain satisfaction in bad ideas being whittled away since that is itself a reflection of the scientific process. It just takes a long time for some stubborn ideas, because they have failsafe mechanisms such as the greatest rewards and threats in human conception (heaven and hell) which bribe people towards belief. Moreover, there are practical and psychological benefits, arguably, to such belief, even if they are, at base, illusory. Control, sociality, morality, explanation. Religion can fool the believer into thinking God can help solve or explain or provide these things.

But she really doesn't. It's not there. He's a culturally plucked bunny from a cosmological top hat.

However, when that illusion is found out, or explained by a simple Google search, there is a hole which needs filling. A void. At least, there is for those people who once had "God" doing the job of filling those gaps. For some of us lucky enough to grow up in apathetically nominal households, we could grow up and learn how to flourish without God, lighting up the darkness inch by inch as we grew inch by inch. But others? Others grew up being spoon-fed God, both medicinally to cure ailments, and preventatively, to protect and immunise them from the dangerous threat of non-believers, other-believers, sort-of-believers and slightly-different-denominational-believers and their more obscure uses of critical faculties. For these people, to lose God is to lose important parts of the cosmological, social, moral, philosophical, explanatory and psychological jigsaw.

Atheists and humanists who have come from previous religious backgrounds have had to rebuild that jigsaw, to create it themselves. This volume of poems is part of that jigsaw. Poetry

4

can be both the cathartic process of shaping that jigsaw as well as the picture itself. A means to an end and an end in and of itself.

The poetry in this anthology has been for some writers a reflection of the journeys that they are still on. There are poems about the memories of religion, scars that are only partly healed, or indeed fresh and open wounds. This poetic voice is an aspect of that healing process; it staunches the blood loss, or acts as a poultice to reduce the risk of further infection. For others, that journey is over (well, for the time being—you can never be too sure: we humans are fickle creatures) and as such, their poetry is about a destination newly arrived at. For others still, like myself for what it's worth, there really wasn't much of a journey at all. Lucky enough to have lived in close proximity to the destination of non-belief, poetry can be an interesting medium with which to express ideas and philosophy, feelings and sentiments regarding God, and the associated scrapheap of theories.

There is something quite quirky about a creative art form being used to express scientific theories or ideas. Such incongruities are ripe for a project like this. The subject matter of the poems, though connected by an obvious thread, are widely varied. God's characteristics, secular morality, organised religion, critical thinking, death and the meaning of life: there is a plethora of ideas and content covered within these pages.

This is, by and large, a collection of modern poems. But what of the early pedigree of sceptical poetry? In a previous book that I edited, *13 Reasons To Doubt*, Peter Ferguson wrote in his chapter on the history of skepticism:

> Abul ʿAla Al-Maʿarri (973-1058 AD) was a blind poet, philosopher, and religious critic, and most notably a rationalist who valued reason over dogma and superstition. He recognized that religion was completely fabricated and rejected any concept of divinity. He also believed that religion benefited nobody but those in charge and their priests. His poems are small and easily

digestible, and accurately and concisely convey his views on religion....

In his poetry Al-Ma'arri tackles many facets of religious belief: he dismisses an intelligent creator, disregards any notion of an afterlife, highlights the falsehood of rituals, ridicules the intelligence of all the religious regardless of specific faith, and argues that the priests profit from their deceit. Al-Ma'arri is also the only person discussed in this chapter who verges on atheism. Due to the lack of scientific knowledge it was impossible for people to conclude there was no god. In fact, we find rather few atheists in the modern sense until the 20th century, when there was finally enough data to discount the possibility of a god. However, by dismissing the concept of a creator in one of his poems, Al-Ma'arri has come pretty close to the premise of atheism.

I will include some of his short poems later in the book.

Within this anthology, the styles of poetry differ vastly. There will be some pieces to your liking, and no doubt others not so much. There are some that are obvious, and others that will leave you re-reading to work out what they are saying. That is the subjective reality of such a creative form. This might well reflect the different types of minds at work. There are those of us who are deeply rational, scientific or even digital in some sense, whose poetry might well differ from that of a more, dare I say, artistic or creative mind. But those heathen subjects and conclusions are the same. Some are from seasoned poets who have refined their skills over time, and others will be from amateurs who are somewhere on their own artistic odyssey. That is the nature of taking submissions from such a variety of places and people, but I think it all adds to the rich tapestry of poetic threads.

I hope this collection chimes, if not fully, then in parts, to a frequency which resonates to your inner core. And perhaps, in a week or two, you might find yourself on a train, in your office, away on holiday, or stuck in a traffic jam, penning (or speaking into your smart phone) some expression of your feelings towards that often dangerous idea that is God.

And yes, it's just an idea. And yes, look at the world around us now; that idea can be very dangerous.

Part One

God (and lack thereof)

God is a complex set of characteristics and properties, and these properties don't sit well with each other. Omniscience, omnipotence, omnibenevolence, omnipresence: these apparent properties are problematic when embodied in the same entity. Readers might well be cognisant of thought experiments and arguments such as the Euthyphro Dilemma or the Problem of Evil. The idea that God is both all-loving and almighty causes issues when understood in the light of suffering, and the sheer weight of suffering at that.

There are other problems too. God cannot be all-knowing, because he wouldn't know that he knew everything, that there couldn't be something unknown to him. For example, we don't know that our brains aren't in vats and having stimuli plugged into them, that we aren't living in The Matrix—we take these claims on something like faith, or an axiom. In the same way, God couldn't know that God wasn't in some divine version of The Matrix, that there wasn't some greater God pulling his strings. God can't know that he knows everything.

If God is perfect and all of his decisions are, by definition, perfect, then the decision to create this world is in some way perfect, given his supposed omniscience and knowledge of the outcomes associated with this world. Ergo, this world must in some way be perfect. Which appears, with cancer, genocide, plate tectonics and whatnot, to certainly not be the case.

So on and so forth. This violent god appears not to be endowed with the characteristics claimed of it by its adherents. That is much of what this section deals with. Who is this God, and how can he be such a wonderful role model when he does the things he does, allows the things she allows, or designs the things it designs?

This frustration that believers feel is often the first port of call for the growing sceptic on their journey to disbelief. Questioning the world around us in light of God's supposed characteristics is a good place to start our own poetic journey.

Eulogy

God died today in the heart of another man.
Ashes to ashes, dust to dust,
And in this soil a seed is planted.

God died today in the mind of another woman.
The black dirt, the moist earth,
From this new garden, wisdom grows.

I was always taught that God died that I might live.
I never realized how true this was.
His death nourishes the seeds of wisdom, happiness, and freedom.

This is a eulogy, a benediction.
I am saddened by my loss,
But know a better life is ahead of me.

Love and hate marked this relationship.
I loved this mythical invisible father.
I hated the crotchety old judge.

Like the child of an alcoholic,

Or a battered wife, who still loves her husband,
I am glad he's gone, but I still miss him.

The new garden I have has wonderful plants,
But I still have to pull weeds of doubt and guilt,
It's my responsibility now.

As a child must grow and leave the safety of home,
I have grown and left the eternal security of heaven.
I have outgrown my god, and laid him to rest.

Bill Barnes

Inimical

The most dangerous enemy
Is the one you don't see
Microbes are enough
Why do you want gods?

Mitchell Cole Bender

Atheist

I'm not supposed to tell you I'm an atheist.
You might be concerned I have no moral compass,
no certainty concerning the finer points of the universe.
Better to dress it up and affect Taoist,
Plump it up and claim agnostic—gush
Gosh, wouldn't it be nice to know?
Make of God such a windy abstraction
one might as well pray to the wind,
but please don't say that word.
Sorry. I love life, Earth
its glorious habitat, sailing
through space, teeming with intelligent
faithful killing each other to confirm
which speaks for God. In silence I am
still mindful of our course,
our vessel,
the frailty of the crew,
its rare and precious cargo.

Dennis Danvers

Serious Clown

I doubt the fact that there could be
a downside to ascension,
It's something that I've said before
but just forgot to mention.

I believe that atheism
is the only true religion,
I'm not certain but I think
this maybe my decision.

I sometimes think I'm always wrong
but mostly I'm never right,
and I think that I'm intelligent
but I don't think I'm too bright.

I never think about my thoughts
just assume that they are true,
and always try to learn about
something I always knew.

I'm happy just to be myself
and I never wear a frown,
I wouldn't change for anything
I am the serious clown.

Norman Littleford

Your Gift Gorgeous,
or How Handsome is Your Boat?

"An eye for an eye, a tooth for a tooth"
once wisdom
now a Fool's Game
the Male Mind now a desert
thirsty, starved
without any notion of wetness
or the pale blue invitation of water
what some call awareness.
Instead, only horror
severed families
blood all over religious fanatics
now run amok
killing each of God's rare
Ancient Creations
that were not like them
their "god" a ferocious policeman
judge, spitting maniac
gun-totting general—
not grateful Poet or kind Father
nurturing Mother or colorful Creator
that gladly holds every one of them
all of the Kingdom
all that Variety
equal
equally tight.

Thank God for their melodic instruments, songs
and grateful prayers
because little did each of these old, cemented religions
worship God's Full Family
Six Billion Year Creation
the Fatness of All the Animals, the abundant Colors of Nature

the Variety of Cultures
every single thing God, or Nature, actually put here
the Bananas growing, the goat milk given, the Humor free
the Christian's Grace, the Muslim's Prayer, the Buddhist's Breath
this almost fanatically Varietal Creator
known for more species, more culture
more intelligence, more science
more thought, more understanding
not less.

Instead, the world overflows
with entire ignorant cultures
tight-lipped fathers, ferocious families, battling brothers
the blood of entire civilizations
exacting their unforgiven judgments
now forcing their social or religious laws on you
their Tiny Point of View
indulging their enmity
their hate
their Flag now complete
their Religion whole
their Tiny Unexamined Life
now "All Wisdom."

Their "God" only male, never female—
as Policeman and Judge, not Loving Father or Poet
a Clobbering Battle General
not Nurturing Mother
ready to knock some sense into you
or easily annihilate your entire village
this "God" certainly not even as worthy
as a good friend
or your own mother
who took the time to help show you the way

or offer you everything she possessed.
These Old Intractable Traditions
still overflowing with their spit and vinegar
still fresh on this earth
intent on forcing each son
every wife
each daughter
every Art & Culture
that God has breathed Poetic Life into
to be Them
to do the Policeman's Will
this Male's Bidding
even meddle in all your "stupid" behaviors
after all, "What's wrong with you?"

Meanwhile in the East
or in the Heart of The Poet
or within the Thoughtful Observable World
of Common Sense,
if someone said he was the author of his blue eyes
he was seen the fool;
where he who counted himself the author of his Talents at Birth
was considered a simple mind;
where he who counted his sense of humor his own creation
not gleaned from 6,000 days in the den of a silly father,
was seen an unthankful simpleton.
And what poor little bruised ego
or thirsty insecurity
or ignored thanksgiving
allows one to consider himself the creator of his selflessness
his much-admired care for the poor
after he had lived in the stirrings of 18 Falls and Winters
in the warmth of his mother
and all of those hot dinners and warm coats
she collected for the poor?

So that in the Thoughtful Observable World
or sometimes in Asia
common folk knew something 2,500 years ago
that the Raging West and Mideast still refused to learn:
that behavior was largely the result
of where the Fates made your landing
along with your Genes
your Family Line
your grandfather's artistic touch as well as his huge frame
your great-grandmother's pension for parties as well as her blue
eyes
your mother's raging temper as well as her small wrists;
that behavior was sometimes also entirely the result of Family
Example
what you saw happen during each of those 6,000 Days
of chaos or sweetness
caring attention or complete ignorance of You
Rules and Boundaries or the Spoiled Excesses of Narcissists
6,000 days of fear and survival
or play
a very specific warm or cold or freezing environment
that molded and shaped each person—
that the Totality of You was only very partly in your control
your Will in a Powerful Wind
depending on whether your parents made $20 a year
or $200,000.

Or whether you lived 10 years in the grip of cancer
or lay dying like a million children are right now
or not;
and depending on whether your Family or Village ever planted in
you
a thirst for violence or art

17

for ignorance or reading
a love of craft
or any other habit of self-discipline--or not.
Each of these Blessings, Evolutions and Fates now conveniently
forgotten
a starving, Self-Protecting Ego
now frantically grabbing all the credit
a Tormented Shame taking all the blame.
And yet what Nurturings and Stabbings
of innocent, starry-eyed children
over twenty Winters
a thousand Tuesdays
and yet another thousand weekends
ever loomed larger in the lives
of each person here walking?

So that God was much more Generous
Fate Larger
much more Understanding
of your "good" and "bad" behaviors
your Brand-New Idea
among God's Six Billion Year Creation
that Nature or Fate could be "Bad."
Your brand-new Pre-Packaged Idea
Unexamined Sales Pitch
here on the earth now
after only 5,000 years of "God's Ethic"
Nature's Oceans churning
Fate's Fish having now blown bubbles
for 650,000 years before you ever came
shouting
cementing these Religious Requirements
unlike God
who was much less concerned with your behaviors
than how Beautiful or Unhappy you were

floating there freckled or black
happy or miserable
there among the other Fish
Birds
Whales, Tigers
Mosquitos.

Much less concerned with your behaviors than
what your Experience would be
on your Boat
your Venture
your joyful Gasps at the stars
your Conundrums
your Loves
your Dilemmas
your Lessons Learned on the high seas
your Beauty and Awareness floating here
not the Results.
Nature, God, Fate, the Universe
(along with your Genes and Family Example)
building your Boat
choosing all the wood, nails, glue, brass
the fat sails to sail, the open portholes to see
all the hot oatmeal and fur coats to keep you warm.
Fate, God, Nature, the Universe
choosing most of the Storms
Star-Filled Nights,
Cracked Hulls
even a few of your Kisses
on those clear days of your Adventure.

Indeed, if Nature was the Creator of 100% of your Boat's shape
color, size, contents;

if the God's, or the Fates, were responsible for 100% of your
Boat's
Early Sailings
even most of your Destinations
was it your "good" and "bad" behavior
your "good" and "bad" sailings that occupied God's time?
Or was it the absolute Thrill
the gut-wrenching Experience
the Lessons Learned
on the deck of Your Gorgeous Vessel
this Boat's Color and Strength and Buoyancy
in the Winds of Fate that would surely blow?

Yes, the questions God asked of you
were not about your "good & bad" behavior
as much as they were about
how unique and rare your Creation was
this Evolution, your Drama, this Holy Process, your History
of "Why" these behaviors were there in you in the first place.
It is true that you did often leave her
but wasn't it because she wouldn't
shut-up
three months of screaming would wreak havoc on any psyche
or was it because you were a bad person?
It is true that Robert did steal food
but was it because he was a criminal or because he was hungry?
And if he had no parents to teach him to work, would he ever?
Indeed, was she the "town whore"
or did her father repeatedly rape her as a child?
And was he completely unreliable
or did he later find out his diet was lacking a certain medication?
In fact, didn't you yell at everyone in your family
not because they misbehaved
but because you hated your work
and were oh so tired?

Indeed, here was God, here in this Holy Process
in You
in your Holy Seeing
the Holy Revelation of WHY you were so temper tossed?
Or WHY people could walk all over you?
Or WHY you had to be right all the time
so much more the point
than endlessly blaming you.
Or him.
The Gods certainly unfazed by
all of your quick judgments
condemnations
your lack of compassion
your cheap, lazy cartoons
of "good" and "bad" behavior
and having written-down so permanently
that this is exactly who God was.
Obviously, community cannot tolerate certain behaviors
but will they ever
ever end
without actually understanding how they are born—
us finally Disciplined Adults
not the Crusty Vindictive Lynch Mobs of the Centuries?

So, friend
how much of your Boat did you create?
And how much of the wood and nails and glue did you
contribute?
How far had your Boat sailed before you even began to awake?
Indeed, hadn't you lived every hour of your life on an Ocean
in a Weather
on a Colorful Sea
a Chunky Soup
a Holy Fate

that had shaped and punched and serenaded you?
Leaving you now standing there
sometimes struggling
with your "Good & Bad" Behavior?

Sure, you can sail this boat
but how often does it go where you tell it?
No, you can't control the wind
or the storms
or always whether the land rises to meet your hull
but you do manage to sometimes reach your goals, don't you?
Sure, you can control this boat
but how often?

Do you really think you are smart enough
to have created all your Talents at Birth
or your Temper, your Sentimentality?
Or that you can actually control which person your heart pounds
for
when your chest goes "Bang, Bang, Boom!?"
Or that you can actually control who and how much you love
or hate?
Or, lying there in your first waddling, what Design you would
become
how skinny or fat
you would someday be
what all of your holy history has been
your Life's Arc
your Fate?
Tell me, were you the Master Author of You
or did God build
Nature paint
Fate prepare
You?

So the answer had never been "An eye for an eye"
or "burning in hell for eternity"
or behavior alone
but "Why" you do what you do.
Much more important to
see your Colorful Dramas
your Chunky Dilemmas
and learn from them
accepting yourself as part of Nature's on-going Evolution
understanding yourself as Unfinished
forgiving yourself as God's Child,
Fate's Vessel
one of the Sky's Shooting Stars
out there on the high seas.

So the answer was not "An eye for an eye"
or "burning in hell for eternity"
or behavior alone
but "Why" he does what he does.
See all of his Colorful Dramas
see his Chunky Dilemmas, not just yours.
Accept him as Unfinished
forgive him as God's Child
Fate's Vessel
one of the Sky's Shooting Stars
out there on the high seas.

Indeed, how handsome is your Boat?
Not even what you do with it
maybe something about how it ages,
but that Grand Vessel floating there right now
decked-out in all of its Holy Comforts

Friendships,
Pleasures
a few Dreams
Children
Adventures
Memory
a daily Breeze
colorful sea flags
a worn white bottom
polished brass portholes that had seen a Lifetime
music and laughter sometimes fluttering in its wind.
And how holy you count its Creation
Journey
Memory
Capacity?

And did you know that deep down in every heart
far from where we judge our lives
far from where we persecute
attack
beat-up on ourselves
and God's other Creations
is a flickering
Struggling Light
a knowledge that innately knows
that innately respects
reveres
this Boat as Unique
Rare
this Boat as Gorgeous?

Your Gift Gorgeous.

C.W. Barrett
Pt. Reyes Station, CA (2006)

Salvation

To convince me
that I'm guilty
is not difficult—
I hear that still small voice
of empathy
that encourages me to work
for the good of my pack
and the continuation of my species.
Yes, I've lied,
I've been selfish.
Lay it on thick now:
as I reflect on my humanity,
set up your arbitrary mark
and I just might begin to believe
that I've missed it.
I seek the world's wisdom,
I have priorities that don't include
paying homage to invisible absentees,
I touch myself while thinking of
my neighbor—
I am human, naked,
and for this I suddenly feel ashamed.
Your silver-tongued diatribe
has me cursing my allegorical ancestors
for refusing to live
in blind obedience.
Just like them, I've reached out for knowledge
and for this I, too, should be cursed.
My emotions raw from the whip of guilt,
I seek solace as you play my heartstrings.
What could be more touching
than Mary's little lamb,
slaughtered;
an innocent man, condemned to die,

for crimes you've pinned on me?
I can't stop to think
about the logic
(or lack thereof)
in your Ultimate Lawgiver being unable to change
His Ultimate Laws
(or, for that matter, failing to live by them Himself);
thinking is what got me into this mess to begin with.
No longer wise in my own eyes,
I accept your allegation that innocent blood
is on my hands, and that the only way to wash it off
is to bathe in it.
I'll believe anything—and believe I do—
to lift my spirit from this miry clay
(I'll pretend I didn't see you earlier, pouring your holy water
on the solid ground beneath my feet).
And so it goes, that my guilt becomes love
and adoration:
when a psyche is battered and bruised this much,
most anything looks like healing.
Vicariously you accept these gifts
and you know that soon you'll have me
on my knees,
eating sacrament out of the palm of your hand.
While looking forward to a never-ending reward
doled out by a nepotistic tyrant,
I'll devote my life in service
to filling your deep pockets.
I'll curse my earthly body,
dying to myself daily,
while the terrestrial beings
go on learning, and living.

                                        Karen

Hyperborean

The frost
the snow
the frigid air
the flurries swirling

I suppose it's sort of pretty
if you like that sort of thing

In Oklahoma
people are always so surprised
when it snows
or gets icy
like it doesn't happen
every
single
fucking
year

Spin outs
crashes on the highway
cars smashed into poles
we should be used to this shit by now

I hate the cold
the snow
and the ice

I don't get upset
or cranky
when it gets cold,
I get legitimately pissed
at the world

The fact that it even gets this cold

is how I know there is no god

Madeline Witzke

And is it not
The foulest of all
Foulnesses that God
In sheer perversity
Has chosen now
To die?

Ted Markstein

Message From An Extinct Republic

Which part of the temple to the Gods
should we close to
protect them from
the decay of faith
before the One
comes and takes
everything for himself

Alex Dreppec

The Essence Of Atheism.

I find it strange
that from the mouths
of so many
the word
atheist
comes out with a spitting motion.

True,
it is not an elegant word
such as
coriander
or strawberry,
where each syllable can be rolled
slowly along the tongue
and gently savored.

It always seems
to be in a hurry
to leave the lips.

Like a piece of grist
that scratches against
the soft flesh
at the back of the throat,
leaving deep gouges
and
the bitter taste
of blood.

                                        Black Narcissus

Creator

Oh good creator,
Who made me debater
Of all those who say you are true;

What I wouldn't give
For a life I could live
With a smidgen of faith in you.

S. L. Ackerman

Creation Reveals A Lack of Sense

You said, "A wise one created us";
That may be true, we would agree.
"Outside of time and space," you postulated.
Then why not say at once that you
Propound a mystery immense
Which tells us of our lack of sense?

Abul ʿAla Al-Maʿarri

What A Foolish Race Are We

What a foolish race are we, spending our lives,
peeking around the sides of a mirror,
trying to find the person on the other side.
We leap over the mirror, pouncing onto thin air.
What a foolish race are we, that we cannot see,
that it is merely an image of ourselves.

Stephanie Savage

Perspective

I seriously doubt
that a creature who eats nothing
and shits worlds
cares
if you worship it
or not.

Bob Zahniser

Who Is God?

We are told there's a God watching over us
a theory that has never been proved,
yet millions of people believe in him
with a faith that cannot be moved.

With so many people praying to him
they must think that he is alive,
but we know that everything living must die
so how long can this God survive?

I am not knocking religion
we need it to bring us together,
but no matter how great you think he is
even a God cannot live forever.

If there is an omnipotent being
we wouldn't be much of a task,
if he knew what each individual needs
why would he make us ask.

I'm told God created our world
in just six days, all on his own,
what has he done since and where is he now
and why do we think he's alone?

Norman Littleford

Five Thousand Dead Gods

No god I know is still alive—
all five thousand and seven
appear to have died.

The great god Huitzilopochtli
led the Aztecs' divine pack—
but He departed awhile back.

Zeus was fun, and had His run,
but while disguised as a swan,
they say, His neck got wrung.

Pluto—God of the Underworld,
offended the ladies of Hades,
and got buried in his own Hell.

Thor, I'm told, was big and bold,
but going out without a cloak,
they say, He died of the cold.

And ghosts of dead Indian gods
can't even haunt a decent tepee,
and many die on late night T.V.

No prisoners tremble on the altar
when their beating hearts are torn
to join Tezcatlipoca in the sky.

And no children scream as they
are loaded onto the simple machine
that feeds them to Moloch's fire.

And for ancient Greece's Dionysus,
no drums sound, no flute plays—

but, oh, weren't those the days!

The goddesses, too, we must include,
for all were dear to some, and lived
in our hearts until the time had come.

There was Athena, Gaia, and Kore,
Xochiquetzal, Minerva, and Astarte,
Ixtab, Kuan Yin, and Kali of course.

Five thousand gods and goddesses—
maybe ten or a hundred fifty thousand
or more, there might have been.

But the goddesses and gods have all
gone, one by one, until there are none
but those that are still willed alive.

Gods and goddesses kept alive
by people still believing—still
trusting—in their own creations.

Pinocchio becomes god of the wood,
while Pygmalion falls on his knees
before his goddess of stone, Galatea.

We remember the Loving Mother
and the Father the All-Mighty
looming large in an infant's eyes.

For each girl-woman makes the God
she craves and needs—then kneels
before Him and says, "Oh, please!"

And each boy-man makes himself
a Goddess that he wishes,

giving a Mother's hugs and kisses.

And older men and women tend
to make our gods with
wrinkled brow and constant pout.

Still we always make our gods
to look a lot like me and you—
one head, one mouth, two eyes.

But the god of songbirds flies,
and the gods of all the fishes
must swim through ocean skies.

The god of cattle may be a bull,
or just maybe it's a cow—
I can't hope to settle that now.

But I am well informed by
one who ought to know:
the god of dogs is a bitch!

God laughs? No it is just lore!
The joke's on us—but I'm told
She's heard this joke before!

Kyle Oliver

A Letter Unto Myth

I don't believe in you.
Jesus, the Lord, Vishnu,
Shiva, Loki, Thor,
Horus, Ra, and more.

Today, when I tasted desperation,
I almost pretended at adoration;
to get a favor, to finally find some aid,
I almost lied, almost faked, almost prayed.

To pray to one I know not to be?
Profane, to not only you, also me.
To you, in believing solely for the sake of want,
to me, in changing for the sake of some divine font.

So, even though I hold on to faith's lacking,
grant me just this one instance of backing.
Let me evince the ire behind my shame,
all the hatred behind the flame.

Nineteen poems about the same heartbreak,
about the one girl who's made me truly ache;
more than a tenth of all I've written,
to show exactly how hard I was bitten.

Yet for every one, I'd triple them all:
the woman, pain, poems, sorrow's call,
if I never had to spend another day
with those whose creed I no longer say.

I haven't seen my family in almost two years,
thanks to men with nothing between their ears.
I've never felt more alone, been more betrayed,
never had more regret or larger mistakes made.

Today, I defied them, for what I think is right.

They should have learned that some will fight.
Yet despite my bravado, my perceived cogence, I lost;
just one more injustice, one more line they've crossed.

I thought the one I went to unlike the rest,
before today saw him as different, the best.
Now I understand where wrong was my aim;
I shouldn't have expected aught but the same.

For that was the help I almost asked for,
one small victory against the Corps.
Oh, the chance one time to put it right,
impetus to be, change to incite.

You've always known my stance on your existence,
and to your myriad followers my resistance;
that should stress these circumstances' full weight,
that to you I might, even hastily, think to supplicate.

Andy Sprouse

Looking for God on the Oak Bay Ferry

The girl in the gift store
on the ferry to Nanaimo
is searching for something.

Something rich, not costly,
something that suggests,
more than is.

She doesn't see the sunset, the double rainbow,
the orca breaching in the ferry's wake,
the sentinel deer, watching.

She is searching for something,
something tenable.
Not gaudy, but God-ish.

If she looks hard enough
she thinks she may find it
in the gift shop on the ferry to Nanaimo.

Linda Crosfield

The Bonfire of the Crutches

God being dead and buried, his worshipers now scurry
Pushing and kicking at each another in their desperate hurry
To and fro, they stumble in search of some new crutch
In their fear, in their alarm, in their terror and such.

Somebody should tell them, they can walk unaided
The time for crutches is past, the need for gods has faded
They can run, and jump and be free, they really, really can.
Nietzsche was right so long ago, when he wrote of the
"super man."

And so, today on the anniversary, of the fire on that Campo in
Rome,
That tore the life from Giordano Bruno, but left his memes free
to roam,
The gods are dead, men can breathe, become thinking, caring
people
Tear the Torah from the sanctum, the crucifix from the steeple

Bring your crutches, break them, burn them, it really is not meet,
For a man to depend on a torrent of priests, when he can walk
tall on his own two feet.

Carl S. Wagener
(first published on the Church of Virus)

A Persian Christmas

He was born 25th of December
his was a virgin birth,
they claimed he was the son of God
sent down to live on earth.

Three wise men came with gifts
of frankincense, gold and myrrh,
guided by a heavenly light
to where this event would occur.

By the age of twelve he was teaching
and his reputation grew,
made twelve men his apostles
called them the chosen few.

He performed many miracles
fed thousands with one loaf of bread,
cured the lepers and made the blind see
even raised a man from the dead.

In the end he was crucified
his body was placed in a cave,
three days later he rose again
and his friends found an empty grave.

You may find this story familiar
or you may be surprised to see,
the name of this person was Mithras
and the year was 600 BC.

Norman Littleford

Big Brother Christmas

Old Father Christmas, he punishes those
Who break social rules: the ones we all chose
In an effort to help keep society whole
And he does it with naught but the odd lump of coal
One single day of the year

Or God-Father Yahweh, that nasty old schmuck
When he judges you, you'll be down on your luck
He never learnt punishments should fit the crime
And likes roasting souls 'til the end of all time
No wonder they all live in fear

They might deter those who would lie, cheat or steal
Or they might not, because neither is real
But if one would be so, I know who'd get my votes:
Let's watch flying reindeer, not sacrifice goats
If we must have the Thought Police near.

Mitchell Cole Bender

The Blind Men and the Elephant

It was six men of Indostan
To learning much inclined,
Who went to see the Elephant
(Though all of them were blind),
That each by observation
Might satisfy his mind.

The First approach'd the Elephant,
And happening to fall
Against his broad and sturdy side,
At once began to bawl:
"God bless me! but the Elephant
Is very like a wall!"

The Second, feeling of the tusk,
Cried, -"Ho! what have we here
So very round and smooth and sharp?
To me 'tis mighty clear
This wonder of an Elephant
Is very like a spear!"

The Third approached the animal,
And happening to take
The squirming trunk within his hands,
Thus boldly up and spake:
"I see," quoth he, "the Elephant
Is very like a snake!"

The Fourth reached out his eager hand,
And felt about the knee.
"What most this wondrous beast is like
Is mighty plain," quoth he,
"'Tis clear enough the Elephant
Is very like a tree!"

The Fifth, who chanced to touch the ear,
Said: "E'en the blindest man
Can tell what this resembles most;
Deny the fact who can,
This marvel of an Elephant
Is very like a fan!"

The Sixth no sooner had begun
About the beast to grope,
Then, seizing on the swinging tail
That fell within his scope,
"I see," quoth he, "the Elephant
Is very like a rope!"

And so these men of Indostan
Disputed loud and long,
Each in his own opinion
Exceeding stiff and strong,
Though each was partly in the right,
And all were in the wrong!

MORAL.

So oft in theologic wars,
The disputants, I ween,
Rail on in utter ignorance
Of what each other mean,
And prate about an Elephant
Not one of them has seen!

John Godfrey Saxe (1816-1887)

Part Two

Religion, Holy People
& Holy Places

Atheists and other forms of non-believers (there are always others!) often don't spend a lot of time and effort in their rejection of a god-figure because, well, they see that entity as non-existent. On the other hand, the structures, organisations, personnel and systems of said god-figures are very much existent. Indeed it is these things that the more strident (some might say "militant", though that is clearly silly when compared to actual militant religionists) of atheists often spend energy in reacting against.

Having edited another book detailing the deconversion accounts of people leaving religion, and the struggles (psychological, familial, social and so forth)—*Beyond An Absence Of Faith*—it has become clear to me that those challenges are so difficult to overcome because of their organised prevalence. Whether they be the formal structures of church and religious institutions, or the more informal social structures which surround them and constitute the local community, organized religion is a problem for the disbeliever. The hangover from the religious euphoria, the spiritual good-times, can take a long time to get over, and often requires more than a glass of rational water to cleanse and purge the psychological nonsense and, indeed, bribery.

In other words, deconverting, or just being a long-term non-believer, is often not so much about the high-falutin philosophical arguments and deductive syllogisms, and more about the pragmatic, day-to-day issues surrounding religion, and merely living as a person, being suffocated by such a social and architectural religious blanket.

The church, with its often high ceilings and lofty theology echoing around its walls, can become a stifling place; and environment of soft Chinese whispers that can become stern words of confrontation to those who do not toe the party line, or adhere to unwritten rules of conduct. Religion, in such places, becomes less about the content of beliefs and more about regulation of appearances and behaviour to fit into prescribed norms.

Freethought does not profit or endure in such places. These are not fertile grounds for the growth of enquiring minds.

Memories of such experiences are fertile for propagation of good poetry and I hope that this section provides an insight into, or poignant reminders, of times spent within organisations, social groups or bricks and mortar which can be defined as organised religion.

The Awful Shame

I must expel the awful shame
That lies within this heart of mine
And curse the source from which it came.

This edict holds a weighty claim,
But of my guilt I see no sign;
I must expel the awful shame.

This sentence bleak that would defame
I have no choice but to decline
And curse the source from which it came.

I will not let this tar my name
Nor suffer any fate malign;
I must expel the awful shame.

I will my worth and place reclaim
And to the trash this charge assign
And curse the source from which it came.

You cannot make me take the blame;
It's at this point I draw the line;
I must expel the awful shame
And curse the source from which it came.

Galen Broaddus

My God, My God

There once was a girl, poisoned by life and left alone,
rescued by God, the God of men.
All she knew to do, between the cry, between the moan,
was dripped into her by men, by kin.
From a booth, of truth and hidden lies,
it said if she believed, she'd own the skies.
And far from fear, was hope of happiness,
so she happily believed, hit or miss.
But happiness never came, only mistakes and harm,
and each new problem brought another one.
Happiness waited just out of reach,
as God sucked her dry like a leech.
She stood by a cliff, surrounded by God's men.
Yelling at her, "SIN SIN SIN!"
All at once she fell from the cliff,
she became weightless, no longer stiff,
She looked up as she fell from the lies,
she took up heart, and started to fly.

Audrena Marie

Turkey Day

All the food in the oven
my senses are lovin'
the smell of apple pie,
I'm so hungry I could die.

Family is here
and all in good cheer,
until grandma calls me fat.
I roll my eyes at that.

Politics and religion must be a note
and suddenly we're all at each other's throat,
followed by intruding questions of boyfriends and marriage,
and allegations of baby carriage.

Can this day be over already?
I'm tired of arguing over things so petty;
tired of hearing about my weight
just as I'm preparing to stuff my face.

And then the annual prayer that takes five hours,
I sit in my seat and drink wine and glower.
This good-intentioned holiday of thanks to pay
for me is really "pretend I'm not a liberal atheist to appease my
family" day.

Madeline Witzke

The Tongueless Gospel: Selected Pericopes

"A religion to end
all religions" he said.

"So then, the best one of all?"

"Ha ha no, my sillies,
it'd have to be the worst."

They began to take up stones.

....

"You have heard it said,
'Do what I say god damn it,'
but I say to you,
'Every rule is just a tool.'"

"You mean including that one you just made up?"

....

"I'll tell you tomorrow,
I promise. Then you'll know.
You, me, everything I've said,
everything you're doing.
It's a fiction. It never happened,
it never will. The sacred places,
the holy books, sin and salvation:
bullshit. You'll see. Wait for tomorrow.
That's when I'll tell you."

Immediately, they seized him and cut out his tongue.

...

Then he was raised up. They forced him to live,
to live again. And did he laugh? Yes he did.

"You can never make me real!" he cried hilariously,
but the tongueless one could only form the sound
of the secret words, the words spoken from
beginning to end, the words we repeat at every gathering
and in every gesture, the only true words:

"Ooo nga emvah maaech mueh wiiieeeeeaaow!"

Kris Rhodes

What is Religion?

What is religion? A maid kept close that no eye may view
her;
The price of her wedding gifts and dowry baffles the
wooer.
Of all the goodly doctrine that I from the pulpit heard
My heart has never accepted so much as a single word.

Abul ʿAla Al-Maʿarri

Father

A prayer sits in my mouth
like the film on your tongue
before brushing your teeth in the morning

I absently murmur
along with the rest of the crowd
knowing that the words are nothing
empty
pointless
going nowhere

I sit in a pew with my mother
first time since Christmas
not rolling my eyes for once
not snickering for once
saying nothing about the bullshit of religion for once
but instead
tears streaming

But he
the man who said I was okay
although I don't believe
the man who denounced god
but only if he is not the god we believe in
the man who loves the children, as Jesus would

The man who lost
his only daughter to a car
his only son to suicide

He stands at the front
in his robes
tears in his eyes
saying goodbye to the congregation

I trust this man
I love this man
I respect this man

The oddest person
to say that about a priest
is an atheist

Madeline Witzke

The Two Universal Sects

They all err—Moslems, Jews,
Christians, and Zoroastrians:
Humanity follows two world-wide sects:
One, man intelligent without religion,
The second, religious without intellect.

Abul ʿAla Al-Maʿarri

The Phantom Messiahs

From whence, no one knows, but a superstition arose;
Men came to blows and a cult gained a following in Palestine.
It festered and sputtered
and some men uttered "The son of God gave us a sign!"

Rome embraced the fledgling cult,
and Constantine—the dolt—converted on his death bed.
Was he dropped on his head?
Till then he thought the Sun was God:
only slightly less odd
than believing God died, but isn't dead.

From the east came another messiah, just as much a pariah
as the phantom that arose from Judea.
The two gods clashed, Jehovah v. Allah,
God-son against Golden One, Valhalla vs. Valhalla.

Hellenic progress put on hold,
If I may be so bold, fifteen centuries of humanity
supplanted by pure insanity.
Crusades ensued, rationality subdued,
Enlightenment no longer pursued.
All science and reason and philosophy
replaced by twaddle with names like Islam and Christianity.

Independent of this Battle of the Saviors
Men with particularly bad behaviors burned witches.
It was those same sons of bitches who followed Exodus,
And learned that "God hates fags" from Leviticus.

Humanity recovered after millions had suffered.
And because of these cults of crap, we endured this mindless
claptrap.
Yet the lunacy continues virtually unabated,

despite the tales and dogmas repeatedly deflated.

One can envision a day when humans
universally revere Reason and Science and reject myths with
defiance;
a day when popes and false hopes and superstition
give way to logic and cognition—a dream, a Utopian transition.

Many were ignorant and lost at sea when the cult was born,
But now we're quite enlightened—aren't we?
And really smart, so why can't we embody sanity
and shake the ancient malignant brain-fart
called Christianity?

Michael Paulkovich

It's MY Life

Who are you to tell me
my way of life is wrong,
or condemn my beliefs
even though my faith is strong.

What gives you the right
to dictate what I should do,
just because I look at life
a different way than you.

The world cannot progress
if everyone thinks the same,
so most people bend the rules
but you want to change the game.

Each person's beliefs are different
disagreements are not really odd,
but if you class me as the devil
you have to be playing God.

Norman Littleford

The Lost Soul

Knocking on forbidden doors
Trying to let the sunlight in
Forgetting the ruse of the damned
Those who know no shore
But endless rough, turbulent seas
They have no diction with which
To spread an impassioned heart
But only the tedious guidelines of routine
With a heart lost to pattern
And the same dissonance that shatters
The soul of who they are
They seek not, and they find not
But a tedious difference in a cobweb strand
Hidden in their same, remote corner
Which for them might be paradise
But only in the sense they obtain
From looking at a framed painting
Of a child at play, sitting in a meadow

Kristi Hendricks

The God Machine

There dwells, deep within our minds,
a thought that, in many ways,
we share with our ancestors,
way back in caveman days.

Our lives were short and brutal then,
as we struggled to survive:
we grasped at anything that might
just help us stay alive.

Our elders wove fables
of supernatural beings,
who directed our fragile lives,
all-knowing and all-seeing.

We took all of our wise men,
prophets and visionaries,
and lifted them to godhood,
with the zeal of missionaries.

Gautama was the first to go,
with his gentle ways and thought:
his acolytes worshipped the man,
not the wisdom he had brought.

Sweet Jesus, with his love for all,
and message of personal peace,
was elevated to the godhead
by greedy Nicaea's priests.

Muhammad, the great unifier,
and social engineer,
was glorified by united tribes,
who listened but did not hear.

Thus it goes, on and on,
passed down through the ages:
we disregard the message,
but deify the sages.

We possess a mighty intellect
but are condemned to perdition,
by disdaining common sense,
and embracing superstition.

James D. Fanning

Blood Transfusion

The Bible says that he must go.
Who do you mean, I must know?
My little one, Davey Joe.
Why do you say this must be so?
Blood is sacred God does say.
You heard his voice in just what way?
The Watchtower Society has its say.
But do you know that they are right?
I dare not challenge or venture to fight.
And what of poor Davey Joe?
He dies a martyr, don't you know.
His life force drips into a bag,
Marked "biohazard," so, so sad.
The saving blood is not of Christ,
Uncle Joe might have paid the price,
And lived yet, with Davey Joe, a full life to savor,
Instead the grave for Davey Joe; though he be young, his time is
over.

Lucretius of Minnesota

Once Upon A Time In Assisi

Helter skelter
Spurning shelter
Rolling, writhing
Snaking down
The steep
And winding
Staircase
To the house
Of miracles
Below
Comes halt
Comes lame
Comes deaf
And mute
And blind
Demented
And insane
Sacred
And profane
Hoping
For a miracle
Or more
To the point
The minders
Carers
Carters
Bearers
Hoping to be freed
Of burdens onerous
And lifelong.
Hoping
For a miracle.
Jealously jostling
Thrusting positioning

Choose me
Choose me.
Anoint me
And heal me
O Lord
Can't you feel me
This isn't
The real me
I lust
For your grace.
And the Lord said
Or so we're told
Suffer little children
But for you
Who art
Children no longer
You also
May suffer
Confident
In the Lord's
Promise of
Salvation
In the next life.
So give
Generously
For Peter's pence
Only makes sense
If everybody
Keeps the
Silver flowing
And now
For fast track
Preferment
We take AMEX.
But hold
This is not

What we
Came for
Traversing
The track
Of miracles
Of holy relics
Of sainted bones
So vast
In number
One can
Only marvel
At their
Sheer profusion.
That Francis
Not forthcoming
In the miracle department
Is another disappointment
In the journey throughout life
So then next
We heard that Lourdes
Is really
Where it all is happening
Where the holy water's
Potent and the blind
Are made to see.
So come then,
All ye faithful
All ye sinners
God so loves
That he gave of
Such afflictions
That they really
Must be blessed
Well, enough's enough
At one point
All that suffering

All that pain
All that torment
Must needs cease
Surely if it be
God's will and
Sufficient inducements
Discreetly or not so much
Be offered and accepted
By his middle management.

Ted Markstein

Warm Walls

That impenetrable reasoning
That polite private sneer
That crazy sense of wonder seeping out from the walls
That tower above the nuisance of debate

....and I watch as that seclusion eats away at the soul
Helpless as I tap on warm walls.

That sense of community
That tourniquet embrace
That crazy sense of wonder seeping out from the walls
That tower above our fragile hearts and minds

....and I watch as that seclusion eats away at the soul
Helpless as I tap on warm walls.

Gareth Howells

Crucifix

If you turned me on my side, I'm a gun
without a trigger. If you held me upside down,
I'm a signpost hammered into the ground.
If you lay me face down, I'm an airport runway.
Face up, I've already turned away from the heavens.
I'm whatever you want to see of me.
I'm an object of no meaning until you pray.

Nobody knows what Jesus looked like.
Yet he's bestowed with a beard, a crown of thorns,
and blunt nails pounded into his palms.
I'm two parts wood to one part metal
poured into a mold in a sweatshop.
I wasn't handmade out of love or piety.
Jesus left the factory a long time ago.

Raymond Luczak

The Atheist Man

The Christians hate the Muslim, and the Muslims hate the Jews
The Jews hate in return, for they have nothing they can lose
And the Hindu hates the Muslim, while the Muslim hates right
back
And the Catholics and the Protestants, stretched each other on
the rack

And even in the forests, of the dark lands to the South
Gods are invented, worshiped, and men run off at mouth
Your neighbor is an infidel, an evil, evil man
Hate him, shun your brothers, and kill them if you can.

Ancient man and modern, the one thing they all do
They seek out gods to follow, and teach themselves to rue
All that is productive, everything that's good
Sacrificing hope and life, because gods said they should

And all of this hate, this destruction, this war
Is caused by belief, but of one thing we're sure
There is one thing unites them, as nothing else can
Their fear and their loathing, for the atheist man.

Carl S. Wagener
(first published on the Church of Virus)

Baby Eater

You're my friend, my family
I've know you my whole life
I know we disagree
But words cut like a knife
Calling me baby eater
Though you can't back your claim
Goes to show just who you are
There's nothing left to say

There's no use fighting you
I'll be whatever you think I am
Satan's slave, I'm a monster
Someone that you can't stand

Yeah baby eater!

You are not afraid of me
You're afraid of yourself
A danger to society
Yeah you really need some help
If you think without god
That you lack morality
Then you should just keep your
Fucking fantasy!

What if you lost your god
What if you left your faith?
Would you become a monster
Someone with bloody taste?

There's no way
For us to be friends now
You've crossed the line
Maybe next time

You'll rethink your words
Or just leave 'em behind

Steve & Tally Cass

Heaven

Do you think
you can
buy your way
into
heaven
eat
drink
not eat
not drink
dress up
dress down
pray
meditate
masturbate
celibate
celebrate
dance
murder
make rules
break rules
build churches
destroy churches

quote
misquote
lie
seek absolution
flagellate
torture
congregate
separate
or none
of the above?
If such a place
existed
and you could
and you would
and you did
do you really think
it would be worth it?

Ted Markstein

Fools Awake!

O fools, awake! The rites ye sacred hold
Are but a cheat contrived by men of old
Who lusted after wealth and gained their lust
And died in baseness—and their law is dust.

Abul ʿAla Al-MMaʿarri

This is my temple

I crunch my way through broken shells,
Brittle sand, addled pebbles
Majestic rock columns breach the ground
In one final, flailing, frozen gasp.

This is my temple.

No choirs here,
Just the steady rhythmic ebb and flow
A heartbeat old as Earth itself
Gulls and gentle breeze the lighter notes
Mozart must have heard your dreams.

Yet you are a god of fury!
Who calls it as you see it
Picking and eating fishermen whole
Crushing stone to powder
Kelp and crab lie dead on your doorway
You rage! You rage against the brazen sun.

But listen you will
Patiently, to my stormed thoughts
Allow me to clamber your altars
To sit on your spires
To weep on your statues
My concerns are like nothing
But yet, still you listen.

Whispering gently to me.
Some day I'll understand.

Colm Ryan

Religion

Watching the news,
Running ticker tape of trauma,
Prayers asked for amidst confused minds and hearts,
Nations fall, rulers lead, religions provide shelter or terror,
Sometimes both,
The confusion of creating a society without a higher power,
Can we regulate ourselves?
Without fear of damnation,
Confused texts giving dual meanings,
Stories edited by leaders wanting servants,
Need for power overriding common sense,
People act like sheep,
Afraid to think for themselves,
Others think, but cannot question what's taught,
Asking questions, finding empty rooms of conversations,
Their curiosity a wall erected, shut out.
God has been my friend, the Goddess too, Buddha said hello for
a few years, Allah I have simply read about, Wicca gave me
shelter before the rituals became the rites of church sermons
with flair.
I am Godless,
Heretic among believers,
Tolerated at first,
Feared at points,
"Are you in an occult?"
Literal questions asked over a remark of fate lines
Learning to side step dilated eyes
Staring heavenward,
Or to Summerland,
Understanding the need for security
Rules and Order the elements of child-rearing,
My freedom to think cultivated by parents,
Both thinkers,
One scientific, result of Nuns and rulers rapping knuckles

In stuffy classrooms,
The other raised southern and Baptist,
Evolving once daughters of feminism
Reared their heads,
Exhaling our battle cry of value,
Still stare sadly at faith released,
Parents want Heaven and Eternity…
I still waver,
Energy makes more sense,
Connections and manifestations
A concept of physics,
My religion has fluidity,
Among rivers and deserts,
Shaped by my cultures,
Cherokee songs and myths,
Christian hymns and lessons,
Pagan reverence for natures call,
Wiccan whisper of chants and flower petals spread,
Pixie dust sparkles as I release my hopes, wishes,
Tut universe captures my imagination's hopes,
Humanity becomes my faith.

I am simply a Patriotic Hippie of reason sprinkled with fairy
tales.

Kristi Crutchfield Cox

[It is worth looking up http://www.tut.com/About for more
details concerning the final lines of the last poem.]

Pretenders to virtue
oafish in sanctity
and self assurance
that their
entitlement
is exceptional
and thereby exempt
from criticism
Perpetrating their barbarity
with the mock solemnity
and false certitude
of the morally bankrupt
one eyed honest broker.
Death to the barbarians
for by all the Gods
they are not us
and clearly
does not God
avert his eyes
turning away from them
thus confirming
that they are
as we always
suspected
something less
than human
and surely
not like us
at all.

Ted Markstein

Fair and Balanced Reporting

Fair and Balanced Reporting
Unbiased News at 10
Independent Viewpoint
Rally Cry of Men.

Talking Heads of Justice
Congress Pushes Back
President's State of Union
Lying on Public Access.

Invade a Foreign Country
Protecting Freedom Abroad
Use Women's Oppression as Fodder
While Claiming Oil as Ours.

Gut our National Programs
Cut Individual Thoughts
God's sitting in the White House
Whoever would have thought?

Polls Suggest Uprising
Americans Slowly Awake
When rights are being taken
For one religion's sake.

I wonder when we'll notice
Hypocrisy seems to abound
We're warring against terrorists
Who claimed religions' mound.

And now extreme evangelicals
Meet weekly with our Prez
To dictate foreign policy
Based on a book by men.

Will we ever notice
Before it is too late
History's constant legacy
Of religion endorsed hate?

If Jesus were alive today
And walking down the street
Those who cried
At "Passions of Christ"
Wouldn't even wash his feet.

Our ideology of what's beyond
Is based on stereotype
Of what we choose as our belief
Imposed on other's lives.

Religion is not government
No matter what you say
For even Jesus warned against
Politicians who use his name.

Kristi Crutchfield Cox

What Do We Really Want

We like to think we're intelligent
some people think they are wise,
but maybe we are just arrogant
full of selfishness backed up with lies.

Each of us lead multiple lives
show each person a different you,
we wear many masks in society
even we do not know which is true.

We are always hoping for miracles
take for granted the ones that we see,
the fact that we are alive at all
is miracle enough for me.

If all the matter in the cosmos
represents all the knowledge we own,
at least 90% of dark matter
would equal everything still unknown.

Maybe nothing is really impossible
if there's something you cannot achieve,
try total belief and an open mind
you can do anything if you believe.

So why aren't we pulling together
blaming religion seems so absurd,
for it isn't God's will that keeps us apart
it's the men who interpret his word.

Norman Littleford

Jonathan MS Pearce

Part Three

Prayer

Prayer is the conduit of communication between God and all the believers. Most every theist sees God as some kind of personal entity who listens with human-like interest and understanding. God is a human, really. Believers treat God as such, because we cannot imagine anything other than that, and we certainly couldn't imagine a personal relationship with an entity who wasn't in some way like a human. This anthropocentric anthropomorphism of God started off, originally, with God's body. He had human form, or perhaps animal form, in looking at the world around us and being creative in our God-genesis.

As we progressed through the history of the world, we changed our view of God. God became ever more distant, and ever more abstract. God moved from on top of the mountain, to over the mountain ranges, then into the sky, to outside the universe. Now God is little more than an abstraction.

Yet still there must remain this human contact with God, whether in bed at night, in a church on your knees, in a mosque bowing and genuflecting, before an important match, after opening Christmas presents, or before an important court case, prayer is vital to the believer. However, it is nothing more than an illusion, a piece of psychological necessity for the believer, a comfort blanket, a form of thanks for things that were brought about by fellow humans or the cosmos.

There is nothing more frustrating to the sceptic, the respecter of science, its methods, its successes and its protagonists, than hearing of a mother who has had her five-year-old son saved by a team of eight surgeons and staff pulling on decades of collective experience, hundreds of years of collective knowledge and the latest scientific technology, only to pray to God for thanks for her son's life.

We know, empirically, at least as far as it has been tested, that intercessory prayer does not work. Tests, double blinded and randomised, have been done to show it has no effect (for example, in the context of success rates for heart surgery). Of course, God moves in mysterious ways. You cannot test God.

How convenient.

Some might say unfalsifiable.

Some of these poems take on the form of prayer for poignant punch.

A Prayer

O Lord, Give me strength to do that which I have to do
To do it well and with good grace.

And Lord, give others the sense to know that
I can't do, or be expected to do, everything.

And dear Lord, give me time to relax and
Ponder on the wondrous universe and
All things therein that thou hast made.

And, Sweet Lord, give me the insight to know
and see thee in others and to recognize the thieves, muggers
and adulterers, the perverts, the fornicators and sundry
sinners, and cast them into hell and eternal damnation.

In thy name (of course)
        Amen.

                              Norman Roebuck

God of the Magic 8 ball

Here I am again,
Praying to the God of the magic 8 ball
That I only speak to when I have a decision
That I cannot make on my own nor do I want to

Here I am again,
Asking the powers above that I don't believe in
To forgive me one last time and relinquish
The sins that I have chosen to commit

Here I am again

Chris Mills

My Prayer

Oh God, the next time
You attempt suicide
Please don't settle for just
Pretending you died

Mitchell Cole Bender

Our Intelligent Designer,
Who art in the unspecified-good-place,
Unknown be Thy name.
Thy flagella spin, Thy mousetraps snap,
On Earth, as it is in the
Unspecified-good-place.
Give us each day our unchecked apologetic.
And forgive us our invidious comparisons,
As we smite those iniquitous Darwinists
With rhetoric.
And lead us not into encounters with people
Who ask us to state our theory,
But deliver us from biologists
Who know what we're up to.
For Thine is the irreducible complexity,
And the wiggly parts of bacterial bottoms,
And the inapplicable theorems,
Now and forever.

Amen.

Wesley R. Elsberry

I bent my knee to beauty (Agnostic prayer)

I bent my knee to beauty
and wished for all to see,
it's not in modern fashion
you'll find the missing key.

I bent my head in prayer
and uttered out my plea:
—"God, make all mankind certain
that goodness stem from thee."

I knelt in benediction
and swore a sacred oath
to protect the children
from apathy and sloth.

Though life is fey and wondrous
all men will die alone.
Our beauty lies in living,
at peace with the unknown.

Anders Samuelsson

Oh My God

Oh my God,
I've come to say
Thank you for your love today
Thank you for my family
And the cancer you gave Auntie Eve
Thank you for the little worm
Who burrows into eyes to give blind prison terms
Thank you for tectonic plates
Which make death and destruction a common fate
Thank you for the failing harvests
That bring about death through painful starving
Thank you for the carnivorous food chain
Which results in slow death after flesh-ripping pain
Thank you for HIV/AIDS, smallpox and malaria
Ebola, the plague, cholera; heck, which is the scarier?
Guard me in the dark of night
Which is every day for that girl with no sight
And in the morning, send your light
The burning gas-ball which will one day end our lives
Amen

Jonathan MS Pearce

The Gift

I knitted these mittens
because people like us
know how it feels
to be nothing but knots,
to be unraveled back to nothing—
    a meaningless mess of fiber,
to fear you'll never be redefined.
Because people like us
get a gift from a stranger,
a wave to go first,
an offer to sit on the bus
and it feels like a fortune
or love
and if I have the chance to give that
I will.
I will put my hands together
for every knit and purl,
and each stitch will be a prayer
that you can actually feel.
But even the roughest ones
from the dollar store down the street
could save a life.
Not that you need saving.
But I do.
So I knitted these mittens
for me and for you.

Kim Mitchell Freed

Pray Back

I shout my prayer to heaven, whisper it
Full deep within my heart. I do not know
Angels or God or mystery, it goes
Outward to find what's there. And then, I sit
Silent, in meditation; mindful, quiet,
Serene. I've never heard a message back.
No matter, dearth of a response, a lack
Of miracle or visitation from it,
Isn't the point. The gratitude is all:
Acknowledging my joy inspires a higher
Aspiration—to serve myself and others;
We have, I think, but this one life, this call.
And so, I shout my prayer to heaven so
I hear and heed it, whether no echo.

Christopher G. Doyle

Dear Father

My moral compass sways. All throughout the day.
With the assumptions made, I figure I'll have to change.
Although I show no restraint. This is a growing pain, these
feelings won't go away.

I'd like to ask for forgiveness and pray. But I no longer own my
faith. If I'm wrong, put me in my place. I keep coming up empty-
handed whenever I'm asked to show my faith.

Back when I was too soft spoken to speak for myself, having
someone to lead did me well. I was too weak. People couldn't tell.
And going to church two times a week didn't help.

Until one day it hit me. Had an epiphany, that all religions lead to
the same thing, eventually. One notion like an ocean but
composed of many streams. The most common thing is the lack
proof in their history.

Not to mention the extremes and how we treat our enemies.
One says that we should love them. The other says stick a knife
in their back when you hug them. Or give them the blade, turn
the other cheek and trust them.

Or that women should be totally sheathed in public. The list is
endless and full of contradictions. Therefore, I repent less, laugh
more and condemn stress. I choose to follow logic, not tradition.

I truly hope that God exists but in church we're too focused on
the story of Jesus to acknowledge him. From how many different
angles can you tell it? And abuse the law of gravity to make it all
angelic?

Why is anyone who questions you a skeptic and everything you
don't understand associated with the devil? Why do you capitalize
on making your people feel helpless and what you ask for tithes is
men's most prized possession?

Why did you hypnotize my grandmother into teaching this as a
lesson to me in my adolescence to adapt to stressing? Besides all
of the minds you controlled. When I was lost, you gave me faith.
In the dark, you gave me hope.

Still, within this lifestyle I did my worst. Knowing I had someone to drag me out of the mud when I did my dirt. I don't need a Dr. or diagnostic. I was born a sinner, raised as a Christian but I'll probably die agnostic.
Am I to be labeled a useless cynic because I believe more in the influence of a hallucinogenic than the resurrection after his crucifixion? It's gonna take more than a book written by man to prove if it's truth or fiction.

Qualon Fort

The Worst Idea Ever

Dear God,

You truly are the Worst Idea Ever.

Because of You, millions have gone to war.
Millions have died, because of You.
People torture In Your Name.
They inflict cruelty and suffering In Your Name.
And You know the worst thing?
These killers, these torturers, they sleep peacefully at night
Because of You.

You give us False Hope.
When it works out, you steal the success for Yourself.
When it doesn't, we shoulder all the blame.
Instead of responding to Injustice,

You say, "It'll be better in the next life".
Or even worse, You say we will Burn Forever.
That's a nice touch, God.

Because of You, whole groups of people
Come in second place,
Or third place, or forever last.
You don't much like difference, do you God?
But money, power and privilege? Ah. That's different.
Now I know your holy people say otherwise
But we all know how it works out.

So do us all a favour.
We can get by just fine without You.
We can sort out our own problems.
We can talk. We can compromise.
We can understand.
We can dream.
By listening to ourselves, and less to You,
We've made things better.
We've brought light to dark places.
And comfort for crying eyes.

You know what?
We can take it from here.

So do us all a favour, God.
And begone.
You were never such a Great Idea in the first place.

Colm Ryan

Can A Song Be True?

Some cultures chant
melodic circular words
to find their inner-peace
or a needed break
from the never-ending pokes and jabs
the tugs of modern life.
Some bow their heads and hearts to pray
or raise them up high to sing
or close their eyes to meditate
while some work and sweat on fences in the sun
or read poetry in the wind-swept outdoors.

Some blow long slow breaths
in angular yoga poses
or while swimming flat, glassy green oceans;
while others fly huge, cloud-studded skies.
Others dizzily dance and whirl in circles
while still others just memorize
the tenderness of a kiss.

I sometimes find myself
daydreaming for moments
of once again jumping
headlong
into one of these Holy Prayers
bathing myself anew
now washing me clean all over again.
Within the fury of the human brain
it is only the Repetition of Your Passions
of these Truths
these Verses
the glorious repetition of those few
Holy Prayers
that we already know

that can summon
that specific Washing,
the salvational inkling
or thunderous gushing
of that Wonder
those Feelings, Aromas, Colors
those subtle or glorious Sounds
Elations
that longer Peace
that can deliver us safely Home.

But just because you've heard this Truth
felt, seen this Affection, before
means absolutely nothing, until experienced again.
This is why we chant circular sounds
hike or run forests
ponder or pray
work on fences
read heart-felt stories
swim flat oceans
even play
or sing Cash and Beatles songs
one more time.

C. W. Barrett,
Pt. Reyes Station, CA (2013)

Baloney

My delusion has a praenomen; it's J-E-S-U-S,
My delusion has a cognomen, it's C-H-R-I-S-T,
I pray to Jesus every day,
And if you ask me why, I'll say. . .
'Cuz Christianity has a way with F-A-N-T-A-S-Y.

Michael Paulkovich

[For those not acquainted with 1970s American TV adverts, this last poem is a parody of a famous baloney advert featuring a small child cutely spinning out a little food-based dit. It will have particular purchase to those who recognize its genesis. Google it.]

Part Four

Death and the Meaning of Life

The inevitability of death has frightened and challenged people throughout time. It is the one thing we universally seem to struggle with because, no matter how hard we wish and we try, we cannot seem to evade it. That said, we may not even want to, given some deep thought about it, since, as some philosophers will tell you, eternal life would lead to philosophical boredom and this is an interminably bad thing.

In other words, an eternity in heaven is perhaps not what it is cracked up to be. We need death, maybe, to make sense of our lives, or at least to give some urgency and meaning to the finitude which we face.

But still, death preoccupies us all in some way and at some point. We are afraid of it, of that endless void, of not being. Because, for naturalistic atheists, that is what awaits us and there is little comfort in that. Believers get the comfort blanket of heaven, which seems to apparently justify any number of ills and baby deaths; an eternity of paradise. As Jim Jefferies, Australian comedian, quips of heaven (WARNING: ripe language ahead): "And what's meant to happen when you die and go to heaven? You see a big bright light; you go towards the light. What's at the end of the light?... All your dead relatives. Well whoop de-f*cking doo! Did you ever spend a weekend at your grandparents' house? It's f*cking sh*t!"

So heaven may or may not be all it's cracked up to be. Well, actually, let me rephrase that: heaven doesn't exist. So we need to get used to the idea that when we die, we die. We become other things as our body transforms biologically and chemically. Now,

93

admittedly, this makes death a hard sell for atheists. There is no carrot to reward us, no security blanket to comfort us, no promissory note to bribe us. Death is final. That is the joy that atheism can bring to the table! On the flipside, it makes our lives finite, and gives us a motivation to make the most of it whilst we can. We have impermanence; that much is true. But we can outlive our mortal lives in memories of others, in contributions to society. Yes, eventually some universal heat death will put an end to even these things, to knowledge as we understand it. We can cross that bridge, though, when we come to it.

Here, though, are some really worthy contributions dealing with that time honoured tradition of death.

The loss of Illusions (Unbound by purpose)

I died one day on a lonely shore.
Apart from God, I fought my war.
Objective purpose was my bane—
a sad illusion fraught with pain.

—"Oh, silence! I still hear your cry!
Your shout is everlasting,
its sound level is blasting.
Soothe my pain as the night comes nigh."

Bereft of talent and drenched in sin;
unworthiness had worn me thin.
I stripped my soul and laid it bare
and flaunted all my deep despair.

—"Oh, solitude! I hear your roar!
It drowns my anguished gasping
which tears my voice to rasping.
From soul to soul your voice will soar."

From tears to laughter at breakneck speed
madness made me protest and plead.
Beneath me grains of sand cohered—
my tears the dried out beachhead smeared.

—"On Golgatha the gale winds blow.
No man can live with wondering
if life's a frantic, blundering
wildfire—with a fading glow."

Anders Samuelsson

The legacy of life

I've packed my stuff and left the house
The lights are off, the doors are locked
And the key? It's not under that little rock, any more.
I ain't coming back;
I never had the knack
for that supernatural crap.

Whether I'd had enough
Before the tap root of my tree of life's sap ran dry...
Who knows?
What I ask is that you use my bricks, sticks and hay
to build something, starting today:
Anything that can grow and foster hope
Anything to make this space we live in better able to cope;
a finer place.
No one likes to leave without a trace, after all,
so make this useful, embrace life and face it head on.
Whether it be taking some words I've written or said,
putting them to good use, making a pledge
or whether it be paying it forward,
not just empty words, but actions
(they speak louder, haven't you heard?).

So how do you do this good?
you ask, spurred on, stirred.
Do three great kind things to people around you
a stranger, preferably, as a rule of thumb
so it becomes about the act and not
a bass drum announcing what you've done.
Keep schtum, and ask they follow it on,
and on and on—three times, not one.
We need to break the sad, the mad, the bad
and make this society the best we've ever had.

I know I'm just a cog in this mighty world,
this magnificent ticking machine,
a mechanism only partly seen
by our keen, marvelling eyes,
but together we can realise the opportunity we all carry
to build bridges between the haves and the have-nots.
Don't tarry, leave here and spot that chance to mine the quarry
for the riches of goodness:
hey, it ain't easy, but just act morally.
Don't be sorry, pick yourself up and do better
be better.
Don't just seek for glory
(take it from me, you get boring).

Now I've played my part in the lives
of my wonderful family who survive me
who would drive me
day upon day in their own different ways
and whose love is second to none.
Don't worry, I won't bore you; for them I've got another one of
these—
suffice it to say that I hope we have moulded
a pair of boys, emboldened to challenge
and fight for what is right
and use the might of their minds
to carve out lives that remind others
of what possibilities can lead to:
strong and independent and finding their way through
life to knowing who they are, lit by the resplendent light
of knowledge and our love.

Now, I've done what I've done,
did some shit, had some fun.
Look, it's there, on the map:
my journey laid out, unwavering, but I never felt trapped.
Perhaps there were things I could have done more of,

less of,
been more attentive to, or
not made a mess of...
no... for sure.
No regrets, I don't like to keep the score.
As with you all, I've opened up doors,
played my part in the intricate universal jigsaw.
Yada yada yada, Okay, stop that yawn.

What's the point of what I am saying, of this plea?
I know that whatever is me
will die with your memories, which will fade, you'll see.
I get it, that's life, or death as may be.
In these words, and others, I live for just a little time
Perhaps a touch more than those on your lips
This is my legacy: your memories, my writing,
this rhyme.
To do nothing now, after reading this,
well, that's a moral crime.
Do better, be better,
remember this open letter
pleading for you to climb,
pulling humanity with you, though it's no burden,
it's a purpose, your purpose in life's crazy circus,
daring to go on, together to mighty heights.

Is humanity the apex, the paragon of virtue,
an evolved organism of wonder, of truth-seeking
that nothing else is equal to?
I don't know, to find that out
you might need a judicial review,
because it could be construed to be untrue
that humanity's all that and a bag of chips right now.
Who cares what's now, it's already been and gone
All that matters is the course you're on,
where you're going, what goal you're set upon.

Let this be the domino that knocks yours;
rocks your foundation, then sets out the floor
on which to build your bricks, sticks and hay
that create your edifice of betterment all the way
to somewhere new, somewhere great
of harmony with this diverse world of humankind and beast
which of late seems so perilous, but not yet deceased.
You're a part of your fate, and my final thing to state
is that you own it; your life is for you to author:
think before you write
do it with a good pen, with clarity, and share your ink
because you'll blink
and it'll be gone.

Jonathan MS Pearce

Time

Time is not pitiless
Although it flies away
It carries off the woes and cares of yesterday

It robs, it enriches us
It heals the tired mind
It bears us on relentlessly
So we're forced to leave behind
The dust and debris of the past
The ruin and the pain
And in soft and quiet waters
Refreshed, we start again.

Norman Roebuck

Apocalyptic Love Song

One day the sun is going to die
For us it means no more sunsets
To the universe, just one less star in the sky

Almost all who ever lived, have already died
Countless stories of love and war and hope and pain
Now lay silent side by side

And yes I understand that my whole life is just a blink of an eye
in the history of the earth, as with each moment that goes by
but this moment that I'm with you
It feels like time has stood still
It feels somehow like it matters
And that it always will

In one billion years, the oceans will dry
While somehow life may continue
It will not be known to you and I

To think we are so important, is an obvious crime
We know that we are specks on a tiny dot
Hurtling through space and time

And yes I understand that my whole life is just a blink of an eye
in the history of the earth, as with each moment that goes by
but this moment that I'm with you
It feels like time has stood still
It feels somehow like it matters
And that it always will

Shelley Segal

State of Grace

Such is this life that we have won—
one minute here and then just gone.
Through starlit lands that fade to gray
the pain of loss led me astray.

It is the greatest grief of man
to know that loves eternal span
must be expressed within a space
of life and hope—a state of grace.

This is the only life we've got—
one minute here and then it's not.
It is not given you to know
when life will lose its one-time glow.

Like summer rains that feed the leaf—
our time alive's so very brief.
Keep those flowers upon your brow
and know the fairytale is now.

Anders Samuelsson

Gard'ner of Death

I oversee the land that grieves;
acres of lawn and fallen leaves,
prolific mounds of mother earth,
pregnant mementos of rebirth.

Manicured, undulating, hills
mask the role terra firma fills
to swallow mortals in her loam,
their destiny and final home.

And as they slowly decompose,
their longing rests in He who rose
spurning death and burial shrouds
beatific, through parting clouds.

As for me, the gard'ner of death,
I prune old vines and baby's breath
wielding the very pruning knife
I use to trim the tree of life.

Jim Ashby

Collision course with death (From the spirit of a young soldier)

Do not grieve, mother.
It was meant to be.
The death of youth came
quick and violently.

Do not sit bereft
on my window-sill
pleading at the stars
for the living will.

Find strength in that deep
clear fountain within
that gave me laughter
and barn tales to spin.

Do not grieve, mother.
We're death´s absentees.
On these mortal shores
like dragonflies in autumn.

Anders Samuelsson

Death's Debt is Paid in Full

Death's debt is then and there
Paid down by dying men;
But it is a promise bare
That they shall rise again

Abul ʿAla Al-Maʿarri

Epitaph: After Nikolai Ostrovsky

Our dearest possession is life
And since we can exist but once
Live so as not to be seared
By the shame of a cowardly or trivial past
We must live that dying we can truly say
All my life and all my strength I have given
To the finest cause in the world
The liberation of humankind

Yes, life is most precious
It comes once only
We seek significance, not shame
So, Comrade, live each day to earn this epitaph
"The power that I had I gladly gave
To liberate the poor
And end oppression

My flag is red
My country the future
My religion the kindness in human hearts".

Tom White

Manashes

The nurse said, "A week," and we came;
the nurse said, "Today," and he left.

So ended our winter of uncertainty.

This equinox was sacred.
A perigee moon, a solar eclipse,
and a diamond ring.
Our little life is rounded.

It's time to unpack some words from shrouded storage:
words like unbidden and stalwart,
columbarium and fortitude.
Relief.
Release.
Peace.

Words like "My father's house."

These words have a time and a purpose.
They are ours for as long as we need.

The tempest will pass,
and another season arrive.

Carol Colby

People Live On

People live on in the things they do the words they say and the skills they use
People live on because we love them so much; life changes as we change

People live on the places we live, changes we make and the ways we give
People live on because we want them so much; life changes as we change

People live on in legacy from impressions made and community
People live on because they leave their mark; life changes as we change

People live on in the things they do the words they say and the skills they use
People live on because we love them so much; life changes as we change

A hundred years seems so short
Fifty years a crime
But life is a stream of bodies mingling, defying the cruelty of time...

People live on because they leave their mark.

Gareth Howells

Speciousness

My feet are planted firmly on this earth
the stars you see are just mendacity,
I've known it since the moment of my birth
what can't be touched is true dishonesty.
There are no gods or ghosts, just speciousness
that people crave to fill their empty lives,
I view these things as just facetiousness;
'tis sad how man's deceptiveness survives.
No angels fly the rhythms of the night
there are no devils, only man's deceit,
there is no blinding, revelation light
just hopefulness that never was discreet.
In death I'll find the nothingness supreme
the nullity of nowhere's nowhere dream.

Black Narcissus

Requiem a la norm

When I am dead
I want it said

He went without fuss or bother
"Don't hire the clergy here" he said
"I'll meet my God tomorrow".

Just take me to the 'Cremmie'
No flowers, no service, No fuss.
I would like, if it is possible,
For the coffin to go by bus.

Friends could travel with me
And I would pay the fares,
Geriatrics, left—inside
Youngsters, up the stairs.

My box, recycled cardboard will do to carry me,
Just because I'm no longer is no excuse to kill a tree.

I don't want a stylized funeral,
A kind of package tour,
"Travel Thomas Cook to Heaven" would be an awful bore.

So pack me in my cardboard box,
Tie it up with rope,
Leave me at the Cremmie,
I won't get lost—I'll cope.

Collect my ashes quietly,
Take them to Stokes Bay
Shake them out and let them fly
There's nothing more to say.

TAMAM SHUD

Norman Roebuck

Blasted Faith

Death-face unchanged when eyes snapped open,
Bad faith dipped him in a foreign ocean.
Peeling flesh on a mouldy slate,
Features rearranged yet still innate.

An afterthought for him to visit...
Preaching never made implicit.
He lied for her and paid off death,
She wanted all but banished breath.

Bullets ripped on through his chest,
Deception, she gave him her best.
He dreamt it was his final chapter.
Nothing then and zero after.

His blue-crusted skin felt warm again.
He gave her to the count of ten...

Glenn Andrew Barr

Patent Protection

Artificial dummies
Walking down the street
Constructed from the pixelated thoughts
Of a computer genius
Or the mind of capitalism
And ego-centered breakfasts

Clang their glasses
To their empty hearts
And hope that their fill
Is enough to feed their souls

Patented ideas override the balance
Of the human mind
It goes to work
To achieve a dream
But instead, protects itself
From human need

Work those cogs, mind those wheels
Help me devise a plan
I have an army to steal

Create my logo
Mind my plan

Kristi Hendricks

Afterlife

Follow the guidebook for an afterlife
Which one do I try, which one do I try?
I'd like to believe that I'll never die
But I can't comply, no I can't comply

All the self-appointed representatives of their own
imaginings in the sky
They want to usher in the messianic age
They don't mind if it's brought on by nuclear rage

They are so sure of their ability to outlive the utility
of their bodies
But just remember that was the last thought in the
brain of every suicide bomber
in every hijacked plane

Follow the guidebook for an afterlife
Which one do I try, which one do I try?
I'd like to believe that I'll never die
But I can't comply, no I can't comply

Thousands and thousands are humming that the
second coming's coming
And environmental responsibility is succumbing
To the suicidal longing for paradise
Can't we see it's already before our eyes?!

All that makes us who we are we find, cannot
survive without a mind
But you're so afraid to die, you're willing to sacrifice
Living through it all with the knowledge that you
have only ONE LIFE

Follow the guidebook for an afterlife
Which one do I try, which one do I try?
I'd like to believe that I'll never die
But I can't comply, no I can't comply

From the day that you are born, you are going to die
It's not a pleasant thought at all but the way that I
deal with it
Is to treasure each moment with my surroundings
and those I love

I spend my days trying to engage with the world,
To learn as much about everything as I can
Using the body of knowledge which is our shared
heritage to further understand
The historical and evolutionary context of man.

To hold revelation in a higher place is to spit in the
face of those who chose to dedicate their lives to
enrich our own

Follow the guidebook for an afterlife
Which one do I try, which one do I try?
I'd like to believe that I'll never die
But I can't comply, no I can't comply

Shelley Segal

A few moments of life

Transparent droplets
from eyes of sweetness,
first emotions.

We are not yet covered
with an expanse of problems.

However, the storm
of disappointments hangs in the air,
tardy, filled with patience.

It brings a rain of grey hair,
an enormous amount of trouble.

The stages of existence are filled
with new roles, though with gaps in memory
and more responsibilities.

Our close ones depart behind the curtain of death,
life's undeniable end.

Millions of full hours,
watch hands moving manically,
until the cuckoo looks at us.

This last look will take our body,
leaving without emotion.

What is life?
A few fleeting slides; the cross-section of being;
cocktail of happiness, sadness, joy and death.

Norbert Gora

Part Five

Science and Critical Thought

More often than not, philosophers (of which we all are, of sorts) are more interested in how we get to an intellectual destination, not so much in the destination itself. This process, this journey, is what commonly defines atheists in their skeptical worldview... at least in a perfect world, since we all carry baggage, dressed up as cognitive biases, which misdirect us and lead us down paths, which we may desire, but which are not the most justified.

Science, as a method, however, is something that atheists and humanists *do* hold dear. And for good reason. It has a self-correcting methodology (including the peer review process), which means that it is always striving to refine itself (without wanting to give it agency!) to move towards a more accurate truth and body of knowledge. One could ask what religion (qua religious revelation) has added to humanity, in knowledge, over the past three thousand years. No, really, what has it? Because if you compare science with any other epistemological (epistemology is the study of knowledge) method or mechanism, there is no contest.

Take this one step further, and we get naturalism. Let me explain. Naturalism is the worldview that there is nothing supernatural in the world; that everything adheres to the laws of nature in some sense. This can be split into two types: *methodological naturalism* and *metaphysical naturalism*. The former is a basis of the scientific method. Methodological naturalism is the pragmatic assumption that everything in the world works to natural laws. This does not mean that everything necessarily does, but that for the purposes of pragmatism, we must assume it does. This is because if you are doing science, you cannot account for supernatural entities or notions (which are impossible to be empirically measured) as being possible in explaining your data. If I drop a pencil and it falls down, I try to account for that with things I can see and measure (gravity). I do not posit things that I cannot see or measure (invisible, non-corporeal goblins) because that ends the quest for knowledge. It is *unfalsifiable*—I have no way of being able to prove it right or wrong.

So it is not useful to propose supernaturalism when trying to explain phenomena. Methodological naturalism says that since it is no use doing that, for the sake of pragmatism, let's not entertain the idea. It does not say supernatural entities or forces do not exist *per se*. That is what metaphysical naturalism does, and it is a slightly harder conclusion to argue for.

One interesting position is based on inductive reasoning (involving observation). If you were to think of some things which are still unknown or open for debate in what explains them in this world (for example, consciousness and the beginning of the universe itself), then would it be wise to posit supernaturalism or naturalism? Well, these two areas, as *potential* gaps in our knowledge, are often plugged with "God". But this is not a sound conclusion. One analogy is that these two ideas (supernaturalism and naturalism) can be seen as horses in continued horse races. In every previous horse race, naturalism has won over supernaturalism in being the explanation of a given phenomenon. Lightning used to be Thor's wrath until scientific explanations supplanted the spurious supernatural one. And this has happened time and time again. Thousands upon thousands of times over history. And yet supernaturalism has *never* supplanted naturalism as an explanation.

Which horse would you sensibly bet on? One which has never yet won, or one which has won thousands of times?

Inductively, probabilistically, naturalism is a good bet. And the basis of naturalism is the body of knowledge and method which has largely brought about that body of knowledge: science.

It's pretty good.

Incidentally, for those who might be unaware, "Dover Teaches" by Tom McIver is about the Dover, Pennsylvania, creationism court case, decided in 2005 by Judge John Jones, which attracted international attention and remains the decisive legal rebuke to efforts to insert "intelligent design" doctrine into science classrooms. In fact, this section heavily features pieces by Tom McIver who is a long-time studier of all things creationist, and who has mapped out the movement over the years as it has butted against science, and more particularly, evolutionary science.

A Godly Man

A godly man once asked my why
a fool like me could bear to die—
that godly man was troubled much
by needing faith to be his crutch
he was its slave—but I was young
I pitied him and held my tongue.
I'd rather reason with a mind
devoid of faith and unconfined
just seekers on the road, no need
for gospels, psalms or rigid creed.
the answer, though, I now will give—
a fool like him can't bear to live
to bear the cross of reasoned doubt
or stare the door of darkness out.

Tom White

We Are

we
are
oxygen
we are carbon
we are fused from
helium and hydrogen
grown in the belly of a star
born from the catastrophic light
into the might of the universe
beating with the pulse of the stars
on the bridge of a cosmic chorus
four billion years in the making
an underappreciated harmony
of seven billion hearts
in the self-imposed
center of it all
we are

Kim Mitchell Freed

ID's ID
(with apologies to William Blake)

ID, ID, burning bright,
Rescue us from Darwin's fright,
Beastly origin of our race,
Evolution's dread embrace.

But what science or what art
Frames immortal hand, eye, heart?
Can we force religion's claim,
Dare pronounce His very name?

Yahweh, Zeus, or Allah, then?
Yaldabaoth, Urizen?
Raël's ET DNA?
Hosts of deities at play?

Ask the Ichneumonidae
Did he who made the lamb make thee?
Who created Heav'n and Hell,
Human creativity?

ID's ID burning bright
Through obscuring fog and night,
Whether wielding Wedge or prism
ID is: *Creationism.*

Tom McIver

Statement

I was frowned upon
Held as a fool to my own religion
In a neighborhood of non-thinkers
Where I was not Christ-like because of my long hair
Or too girlish that I may send the wrong message (to a panelist
of their own)
Where my mom and I looked too much alike, so she (my only
mom, my only parent) became subordinated too
All for giving me choice

But I still love those smooth-brained loyalists
Where new ideas roll off the brain
And cannot be burrowed by the ugly wrinkles
And so, to me, their grey matter is no matter, absent
For they abase themselves to unnoticed hypocrisy and perpetual
ignorance

Hunter Kettering

From there to here (and back again)

Abiogenesis
A chemist's bliss

First domino
See the Tree grow

Evolution
A divergent solution

Mutation
Variation

Homo sapiens
Sapiens

Wise man
Defies that (think Klu Klux Klan)

God's plan?
He's a man's man

Holy Book, look:
Death and miracles undertook

Humanity forsook
2000 year holiday booked

Enlightenment
No more frightening judgement

Science and space
Advancing apace

War and religion

Intolerance, derision and dogmatic submission

Godsmen have reappeared
We've advanced; why the hell are you still here?

Jonathan MS Pearce

The Flea
(with apologies to John Donne)

It sucked on faith, and now sucks science
And in this flea the two bloods mixed and mingled.
Can these two truths combine
In sacred union—stronger hybrid type?

Well, no, as science claims not Truth
But rather explanation tried by tests;
While faith, if tested never forced to yield,
All scientific fact it can reject.

Our flea becomes instead unholy beast
Grotesque chimera made of alien parts
Of vastly different species;
Both bad as science, and theology.

Be rid of it, this parasitic flea!
Remove it ere it causes strife and grief.
Its death takes naught from God,
Science wins, and so too sound belief.

Tom McIver

Reasonable Doubt

Is there really an omnipotent entity
that created all we survey,
with the power that gave us the gift of life
and the rules for us to obey.

Some say that God put us on earth
just to carry out his will,
but we break all his commandments
even teach each other to kill.

People believe the stories
from a book that's very old,
but transferred into modern terms
a different story is told.

We have the ability to reason
to find out what we don't understand,
but most religions are standing still
only science seems to expand.

Norman Littleford

The Silent Song

The holy land had a holy plan, and it was grand to see
But for all that, it could not be, not as you believed
For judgement, hate, and strife
Became the standard of a spiritual life

Thousands died and millions prayed
Some were bound and some were flayed
And reason, thought, and doubt
Were held up as Evil's clout

Belief is strong; the book can't be wrong
So thought became a silent song
Sung only in the dank and dark
Away from prying eyes, a world apart

But belief gains power from the human mind
So thought couldn't be wholly denied
Only demeaned, despoiled, and decried
        Yet it endured...

Beyond the hopes and fears of faith
A rising tide that would not wait
For the whims of faith and fate
But instead relied on simple taste

To learn, we cried, is the only way
We must improve from day to day
And not cling to distant past
   In hope that change won't come to pass
    In fear of new ideas and a different path
     In hate for the children who long to scream
        'The Emperor Has No Clothes!'

'Paradise exists,' they say, 'Only for those who abide our way

Knowledge is not a toy with which you can play!'
To which we all agreed, 'it is no toy
It is the source of progress and joy'

To deny it to even one human being
Is the greatest crime this world has seen
The criminal is worshiped for all good
As believers die and kill
Trying to make of the world only what they build
For they are right, and all else wrong
While those who doubt continue with our silent song

Dwight Phelps

By way of useful introduction to some of the next poems, Tom McIver writes:

Deborah Owens-Fink was an Ohio School Board member who promoted the "critical analysis of evolution" bill and other anti-evolution efforts. In Board of Education meetings and ID websites she condemned Ohio State anthropologist Jeffrey McKee for a private e-mail he sent to the Ohio Citizens for Science list (our watchdog group opposing creationist intrusions into schools) in which he jokingly referred to Glen Needham and Robert Silvestro of Ohio State as "parasitic ticks hiding in the university's scalp." This was an offhand joking reference to Needham's tick research and stealth creationism. Needham and Silvestro were members of a PhD committee which had approved an education dissertation promoting teaching of creationism in public schools, and McKee had vigorously opposed the secretive and improper way in which this committee had been chosen. Owens-Fink obtained the private e-mails by subpoena, and national ID websites exploited the "tick" reference to condemn anti-creationists.

The Tick

Simple creature, yet complex
In origin and presumed design,
Are we really all related,
Divergent ends from common root?

Should we look to you for morals?
Can you help your loathsome instincts?
Are you sign of fallen nature—
Or evolution's mindless offspring?

Hiding fast in fur, so cunning,
Have you designs ev'n more specific?
Is it your goal to inject within us
Faith disguised as scientific?

We can choose to act with honor,
Approaching truth through science and reason.
To follow blind belief by faith, though,
Is intellectual sin and treason.

O wee critter! sucking blood,
Gripped to scalp, past even squirmin',
At least we humans out-create thee,
Designing God designing vermin!

Tom McIver

To a Sly Beastie
(apologies to Burns ["To a Mouse" and "To a Louse"])

"Teach the controversy"?—beastie!
O what cunning's in thy breastie.
First creation, then ID—disguised
To hide intent.
And when exposed the trick is simply:
New names invent!

We may regret that Nature's judgment
Severed religion-science union;
Belief, though, now must learn survival
With evolution.
Religion shan't intrude in science
Says the Constitution!

ID exposed as creed now—faith-based:
Supernatural in science—wrong place!
The best laid schemes of Wedge and Pandas
No Judge did fool.
Sectarian belief shan't clog or waste
Our public school.

Though ID ploys are now in ruin,
Their devious ways the courts have strewn,
They'll re-emerge with new-coined name:
"Critical analysis."
But this too, would ensue in
Scientific paralysis.

O Debbie, dinna cast out thorns
At critics who protest and mourn
False teaching smuggled into schools.
Political pollution—
Singling out to denigrate and scorn

Just evolution!

O would some Power the giftie gie us
To see mankind as Darwin sees us,
Evolution learned can free us
From foolish notion:
And mindless fear of beastly roots;
Yet keep devotion.

Tom McIver

Stinking Atheists

As Doctor Spandex slowly said
you're dead but then you're never dead
the sun implodes and all will fry
but no one dead will really die,
it's all to do with scientists
who must be stinking atheists
how dare they prove what god forgot
how dare they prove what god did not,
but then it's just hypothesis
another case of hit and miss
or is it truth and do we care
that bits of us are everywhere,
I'll sell my cells for fifty bucks
then cart them off in 6 wheel trucks
or should I wait until the end
when all my cells for free I'll send
like stardust on a windy day
to quickly, quickly fly away
to find another star it seems
and start some newborn baby's dreams.

Black Narcissus

Sanguine in Science

We have put our trust in time
Always asking for appearance
We eschewed truth, doubt being continuous though
Now times have changed
So I beg that you put faith in science
Where knowledge lies
For hope of progression
And a passing of ideas

Bowing to the new entity
With infinite depth in the body
With eternal form and structure
This is the shape of science

Hunter Kettering

Consensus

Consensus, consensus,
There's one thing we know:
What everyone says
Is assuredly so

Oh, the earth, it is flat
And the sky is a bowl,
And we humans each have
An immortal soul

Water can remember;
The stars tell your fate;
God's born in December:
Now isn't that great?

Autism's from vaccines
'Cause Mummy knows best
Never mind those pesky
Empirical tests

Sex is immoral
And dolphins are fish
If I keep making claims, I'll
Sound just like Duane Gish

Aliens among us
Fly in UFOs
We cannot "disprove" it
So anything goes!

Mitchell Cole Bender

Fear of God

Galileo was chided by the God-fearing for observing that the solar system is Copernican, not Ptolemaic. And yet...the wanderers did and do move about the sun.

Newton was chided by the God-fearing for describing all motions with mathematics, not with divine will. And yet...measurements in mechanics could and can be predicted with precision through calculation.

Lavoisier was chided by the God-fearing for explaining chemistry as quantitative reactions, not as miracles or magic. And yet...substances did and do appear and disappear with predictable regularity in labs everywhere.

Darwin was chided by the God-fearing for showing the diversity of life resulting from ecological factors and adaption to them, not from theistic interventions. And yet...life had and has a single structure and has changed and does change forms in time.

Einstein was chided by the God-fearing for demonstrating the democracy of observers, not the absolute God's-eye view. And yet...space and time have changed and do change from frame of reference to frame of reference, and the laws of nature have been and are the same for all frames.

Perhaps the God-fearing are right to fear God. If God is the source of reality, they have been fighting or ignoring God's facts for four hundred years!

Ronnie J. Hastings, Ph.D. (1983)

Dover Teaches
(with apologies to Matthew Arnold)

The sea is calm to-night.
The news is full, the Court rules fair
On ID's fate; on legal fronts the light
Gleams, at least for now; the cliffs of Science stand,
We hope secure, out in our natural world.
Thanks to Judge Jones' ruling, sweet is nature's air!
Only, from old anxieties still at large,
Where reason jolts sectarian hope,
Listen!—you hear evolution's roar
Of evidence consiliently displayed, and fling
The neutral note of science in.

Evolution, through struggle, death, and flight—
But also altruism, love, and joy—
Produced the wondrous world of living things
So beautiful, so varied, and so right.

Plato—later, Paley—long ago
Attempted to deny this natural trend
Proclaiming rather that this ebb and flow
Not misery, but Plan and Spirit do announce:
And also find therein a thought,
That science can approve and render true.

The Sea of Faith
Was once, too, at the full, round Nature's shore
And lay like folds of a bright girdle furl'd.
But now I only hear
Its melancholy, long, withdrawing roar,
Retreating, to the breath
Of old dogmas, down the vast edges drear
And naked fossils of the world.

Ah, Science, let us be true
To nature, as the world we strive to know
That seems so complex, and planned, as if for us;
So wondrously designed it looks to all,
Hath really neither morals, virtue, sin.

Nor final certitude, nor Final Truth;
But science classrooms can't surrender to
Confused religious strife, sectarian struggles,
Where ignorant armies clash by night.

Tom McIver

The following poem, as Tom McIver states:

> ...refers to the 2002 Ohio School Board controversy over proposed Science Standards which IDers tried to influence to require inclusion of if not ID then at least criticisms of evolution.
>
> Jody Sjogren of Kansas formed IDnet with John Calvert and William Harris, then moved to Ohio and joined SEAO to advocate for ID. She is an artist who paints pictures of birds metamorphosing into warplanes:
> http://www.intelligentdesignnetwork.org/Jody's%20Art.htm
>
> Patricia Princehouse of Case-Western biology teaches evolution and history of science, and has been active in opposing these creationist efforts (we both are members of Ohio Citizens for Science, which she has headed).
>
> The strange Indian names are tribal creator gods; they probably don't scan as I have no idea how to pronounce them.

Evolution in Ohio
(Or If Not, then Devolution of Ohio)

Twixt the shores of Gitche Gumee
And Ontario to the eastward
Lies the crooked Cuyahoga,
Famed as White Man's Burning River.
All between the Cuyahoga
And Ohio's westward flowing
Is the land now called Ohio
Torn by fighting for its classrooms.

From across the state they gather:
Cincinnati, Cleveland, Dayton,

Akron, Athens, and Toledo,
Canton, Zanesville, Ashland, Lima,
Youngstown, Bowling Green, and Oxford,
To the Council in Columbus.

Hoping to convince the Council
Ere the Moon of Snow-shoes passes
As the gales of ID bluster.
There to sing of education
Urge the council of our teachers
Help them teach our children science
Not to yield to ID pressure.

From the wigwam and the longhouse
From both scientist and poet
(E.g., Longfellow and Princehouse?)
All our wisest men and women
Urge the teachers in Ohio
Teach good science—evolution.

Also teach the old traditions:
Social studies, art and music
History and—yes—religion.
But do not confuse these studies;
Teach them science best we know it
Not what now is superseded.

"Teach the controversy" say you?
Teach our kids opposing viewpoints?
But why only *evolution*?
Why not all of science also?
All of science had to struggle
All its theories fought to triumph
Some of them are still contested
Others simply won the contest.

Teach the controversy?—maybe;
In its proper field of study.
Let them have their bone to chew on;
Bones can choke as well as strengthen.
Just as wedges can be driven
In our side—or in the other,
Split apart in both directions,
Used by either side, and choked on.

Show our students why creation
Once was thought the explanation
But why science now rejects it
And asks "how?" direct to Nature.
Ussher, Lightfoot (John, not Gordon)
Didn't know of evolution
So they had to query Scripture
Queries Scripture could not answer.

Darwin showed that evolution
Helps explain life's grand procession.
Darwin taught how life descended,
Branched, adapted, speciated
From ancestral life evolving
All by natural cause and process.
Tested constantly by Nature
Science grows, evolves, progresses.

Or, if in the science classroom
You still teach Creation, then you
Must give *all* our people's stories
Equal access, equal freedom.
Not your Bible's story only—
Other peoples' stories also.
Teach how evil Yaldabaoth
Is the Earth's and life's Creator.

Teach the Iroquois Creation
Also Huron, Cree, Miami
Shawnee, Erie, and Ojibwa.
From Manhattan to the Chumash
And all people in between them.
Teach Orenda and Wakonda,
Gitche Manitou—Great Spirit,
Father Sky, Old Man Coyote,
Mother Earth, Sky Woman, Trickster,
And Earth-Diver, our Creators!

Wahkantunga, Sunewavi,
Kohkomthena , Nanih Waiya,
Wheemeemeowah, Yakista,
Tulangusaq, Sitchtchenako,
Gicelemuhkaong, Na'pi,
Yusan, Hutsipamamau'u,
Hahgwehdiyu, Tsohanoai,
Kwikumat, Huruing Wuhti,
Yimantuwinyai, Shiwoka,
Ixtcibenihehat, Quawteaht,
Ioskeha, Taweskare,
All Creators, all Designers!

ID transforms birds to warplanes
While denying evolution,
Trying to deform all science
While denying life's real changes.
ID keeps designing smokescreens
Falsely hiding their intentions
And by wounding evolution
Clears a path for their religion
Into all the science classrooms
Their sectarian creed intruding.

Keep your faith in God *and* Nature—

Just be careful not to mix them.
Don't confuse their different pathways:
Physical and Spirit knowledge.
Nature we explain with science;
God we seek in our religions.
Neither can replace the other,
Both can help to make us better.
Keep religion out of science
Keep religion in the churches.
Teach the best we have for science
Teach our children *evolution*.

Tom McIver

Part Six

Morality and Humanist Ideals

Morality. How many years of philosophy have we endured for this to still be unresolved? Too many. And that's the point. No moral framework is perfect; they all have their problems, and these problems have not been overcome. Does this means morality does not exist? Perhaps (at least out there, in the aether). Moral scepticism is actually fairly hard to dismiss. That said, consequentialism, virtue ethics, relativism, subjectivism, deontology, divine command theory, natural law theory and any other number of moral value frameworks have their advocates and their detractors.

Whatever the truth of any of these frameworks (or indeed none), humanism is the ethical and moral worldview of many atheists. Atheism on its own (as either a lack of belief in a god or gods, or the positive belief that it/they do not exist) doesn't really get you very far. Yes, we may come across the ubiquitous arguments such that Stalin and Pol Pot were atheists and this caused their mass murdering tendencies, but these are simplistic and naïve conclusions based on flawed thinking. At its simplest level, I am an atheist and I do not have the urge to kill people, so there is something more complex going on here. Stalin and Hitler had moustaches, so surely moustaches caused such atrocities?

Atheism dictates nothing outside of the proposition concerning a belief in a god or gods. The morality of atheists, therefore, requires a good deal more philosophy and thought. I will defer to Wikipedia to give a good definition to secular humanism:

The philosophy or life stance of secular humanism (alternatively known by some adherents as Humanism, specifically with a capital H to distinguish it from other forms of humanism) embraces human reason, ethics, and philosophical naturalism while specifically rejecting religious dogma, supernaturalism, pseudoscience, and superstition as the basis of morality and decision making.

Secular humanism posits that human beings are capable of being ethical and moral without religion or a god. It does not, however, assume that humans are either inherently evil or innately good, nor does it present humans as being superior to nature. Rather, the humanist life stance emphasizes the unique responsibility facing humanity and the ethical consequences of human decisions. Fundamental to the concept of secular humanism is the strongly held viewpoint that ideology— be it religious or political—must be thoroughly examined by each individual and not simply accepted or rejected on faith. Along with this, an essential part of secular humanism is a continually adapting search for truth, primarily through science and philosophy. Many Humanists derive their moral codes from a philosophy of utilitarianism, ethical naturalism, or evolutionary ethics, and some, such as Sam Harris, advocate a science of morality

I think this sums up the position nicely. And given these ideals, it is hard to imagine that a secular humanist could become Stalin or vice versa (at least, not without some fundamental changes!).

Leading the moral life is important to many atheists, and one could argue that the tenets of a moral life are intuitively within us, evolved over time, that such a framework is a codification of our moral intuitions. Perhaps. And these are the sorts of debates that philosophers like myself spend an awful lot of time mulling over. Whatever does underwrite our morality and the morality of secular humanism, here are some poems which tap into the rich veins of moral philosophy which flow through the body of humanism.

A Fellow Man

I have no prayers or charms of faith
If God there be, He'll know my weight
If God be nought, I'll still do good
And practice justice as I should

We should not seek reward to do
What decency expects us to
Should Heaven be a kingly court
I'll go elsewhere to prove my worth

Don't get me wrong—I've sought belief
But lust for faith brought no relief
Mere logic leaves me where I stand
I am not blest, nor am I damned

I seek to do what good I can
I am your friend, a fellow man

Tom White

Hypocrite's Litany

By looking where I will, no mirror seen,
I mote another's eye and beam with pride.
While fondling pure with leprous touch unclean,
I damn all prejudice and don't see mine.
I'll be the first to cast my sinful stone,
While smelling rats through pores that stenchly reek.
I sharpen up my tongue to cut to bone,
And talk of love while calling others freaks.
So, deaf to criticism, hearing praise,
I raise myself above the rabblous crowd,
And in my heart I know that I am saved.
"Be quiet, all of you!" I shout out loud.
And Jesus loves me, yes, I know again.
Because my god has told me so. Amen.

Christopher G. Doyle

My Morality

My Morality has nothing to do with the Holy Bible
Or the verses of the Qu'ran

My Morality won't judge you by your spirituality
But by the things that you have done

My Morality is not set into stone tablets
Who don't even tell you not to hurt children

My Morality is not dictated by a deity
It's developed from empathy dependence and love

My Morality accepts everybody's sexuality
Is more concerned with inequality than validations from above

My Morality is not set into stone tablets
Who don't even tell you that
It's worthwhile to be good
For being good's own sake
That not to think for yourself can be a deadly mistake

My Morality is not recitable from memory
It's something inside of me
How I want to be
Treat others how I want them to treat me

Basically not to hurt anyone
Abhors any brutality
It stems from our common humanity
It's what my mother taught to me
It's mine because I'm free

Shelley Segal

A State of Grace

Speak not to me of the grace of God,
or the will of Allah strong.
Don't talk of Buddha's compassion,
or Natraj's eternal song.

No misty-eyed redemption,
nor abject sinner's tears,
with promises of salvation
that prey on primal fears.

No superstitious servitude
demanded by mere men
who put themselves above us
and claim God speaks through them.

What if today is all there is?
No manna, milk nor honey;
no dancing virgins serving wine
in Elysium, bright and sunny.

Let us take responsibility
to live our lives with love,
and not pass that duty
to something "up above."

We can make each moment Heaven,
by doing what we must
to strive for global betterment
on this speck of cosmic dust.

James D. Fanning

Efat (modesty)

You can't avert your gaze
So I must spend my days
Living inside a cage
I carry on my back

You incant his holy name
But still you feel the shame
So I must take the blame
I carry it on my back

You don't like to stare
So much you make it though I wasn't there
Still you take whatever you want

You can't control your needs
So I must pay for the deeds
The horrors done to me
I carry them on my back

What we learn from holy verse
Is that woman is a curse
There's no freedom from this perverse prison on my back
I carry it on my back

Somehow your rights to the divine
Deserve protection more than mine
What will it take to cross the line
For tradition to be called a crime
For my sisters to raise their voice with mine?

Till they can't take what they want

Shelley Segal

147

On Intellectual Expedience

We turn our faces away, time and again,
at media images of death, hate, and pain.
Overwhelmed, problem resolution beyond our reach,
our logical core screams an existential screech.

Wahhabism, ISIS, the KKK,
the faces of evil we encounter each day:
corrupt politicians, and their corporate masters,
serial killers, ecological disasters.

Too many people breeding so fast,
an unsustainable planet that just won't last.
So many realities calling me, me, and me,
so many eyes that refuse to see.

Every tribe seeking to advance their view,
with ethics and religions that exclude me and you:
a feedback loop of stupidity so profound,
that altruism, acceptance and love cannot abound.

We bury our heads, like the ostrich adage,
in the sand of confusion, and ignore the carnage.
Intellectual expedience, driven by fear
of a truth, a reality we don't want to hear.

Well, here's a thought that you might not have heard:
pretend the Enlightenment never occurred!
Let's implement the vision that we all can see,
of a new inclusive world, unafraid and free!

James D. Fanning

Tolerance

They all know God or so it seems to be
submerging in their self-grown piety,
they pray ten times a day which makes them good
and wear such things believers think they should,
it's not their actions but their outward guise
that shows belief and helps philosophize,
they seem to hide the goodness deep within
condemning others to immortal sin,
for me I think they're wrong but that's just me
I'd rather offer actions selflessly
and if there is a God that does exist
my tolerance and good should not be missed.

Black Narcissus

there is a gulf, unbridgeable
infinitely deep, too wide
it seems, for crossing
here is the high ground
the absolute of uncompromise
from whence stems action
or refusal to act
and it is this
despite all the naysayers
the equivocators, the weaselworders
the eggs and omelettes rationalizers
the defenders of the abuses
of power and control
the self-designated pragmatists
the smirking self-assured relativists
the stinking callers up of their
putrid brand of realism
you know them well
you know of whom
I speak
despite all these and
all their attendant flunkies
and oh so smart coteries
of oh so overeducated scions
of cant and incomprehension
despite all these
know that
the end never justifies the means
for here in the flow
of the endless river of existence
there is never an end
to anything

Ted Markstein

Acceptance By My World Family

I thank this forthcoming age
When a man can sympathize
Being greeted always as an equal
Can walk with trend but remain authentic
Appear original in a day of everything
Smile and love all
While a woman can one up any
Be praised for ambition which I find oh so attractive
Recite humane discourses while pondering work
And anyone can find a way to rise
By machine, complexity, endurance on an excursion, in the mind,
or stay stagnant while others fall
All of this constituting a world partnership
With conspicuous intoxication of attraction
So I thank everyone
For being whatever
And creating this day
You made it
No one else
Now I have the ability to be me too
And find a dwelling where I will not be scorned
Or even feel my own internal blows I conflicted before
On thoughts of being a problem
On thoughts of being a bastard
On thoughts of being inadequate
On thoughts of thinking different
On thoughts of being born in the wrong place
On actions of attempt to be me
I think this world and time was meant for me
Because of you

Hunter Kettering

Lucifer or Gabriel?

Legend says we are but that mid-span
'tween airy angels and demons below:
Our nature wrestling itself ever so—
A battle that's between the base and grand.
I've seen no devil from some fiery realm,
Felt no help, no seraphed beneficence:
Perhaps 'tis so and I but lack the sense
To realize such fiddling at the helm.
Within, I feel my own duality:
Scoundrel or saint, that label is my own—
Perceived, I judge and measure all alone;
Fashion belief to make reality.
What clarion call becomes my true life's voice
Is, in the end, determined by my choice.

Christopher G. Doyle

It Doesn't Necessarily Follow

Follow old traditions
that best served another day.
Follow any charlatan
that claims to know the way.
Follow each and every law
our masters claim is right.
Follow superstitious mantras
that may help you sleep at night.

Follow all the game shows,
and reality TV,
and follow self-help gurus
who teach you what to be.
Vote for all the buzzwords
that spin doctors have designed.
Always think the facile thought,
that doesn't tax your mind.
Ridicule but don't discuss
all topics that arise.
Repeat vapid platitudes
that others say are wise.
Look to celebrities
to guide you as you go,
on how to dress and what to buy,
and what you ought to know.

When our lives are over,
and our sojourn here is done,
will we have cause to regret
our short time in the sun?
Will we shed a bitter tear
at a call we did not heed:
why did we simply follow
when we had a chance to lead?

James D. Fanning

Disability

Disability is a random thing,
It affects anybody or anyone;
If you, or someone you know is disabled,
Then you know you're normal, no pun.

Some of us are physicists,
I'm a computer scientist,
Some are TV presenters,
And I knew a secretary, a typist.

We're not a marketing niche,
Which companies aim to target:
A paralysed geek is simply just a geek;
Friendly with other geeks, his outlet.

Society's thankfully not like it used to be,
Ignorant and cold,
People today are kinder and more aware;
You don't have to be so bold.

Stephen Hawking made such a difference to me,
When he wrote his PhD on string theory,
He had the academia's pride and concern,
And caused much religious animosity.

Hawking is one of my heroes,
Because he entitled me to go to university,
To study unaffected,
By a mental illness history, a tragedy.

At university he meant to me
That I could say to whosoever without guilt,
"I am mentally ill sometimes!"
About what had caused me to tilt.

154

I have an axe to grind as I feel rather hurt,
By Christian fundamentalism, so cruel;
So my close friends and wardens knew,
Not to be thus confrontational, the fire to fuel.

Hawking also meant that all are worth it:
Each one has their own hook,
So when he came ordinary folks started to realise,
That disabled people just might be worth a second look.

His book is second most read in the world,
And demolishes the possible accusation,
That disabled people can simply be fitted in,
Rather than welcomed without hesitation.

Dominique Green

Romance

I guess, I guess, I'll guess no more
I don't want your fidelity
And we'll kiss, and we'll kiss, and miss no more
Just give me honesty

They told me about God in the Bible
They told me about Santa Clause
I grew up learning about lies
And how in good clothing, honour
And talking about values
People themselves disguise

I guess, I guess, I'll guess no more
I don't want your fidelity
And we'll kiss, and we'll kiss, and miss no more
Just give me honesty

I learned about how I hear deceit
And I grew up but grew no wiser
I realised what I didn't know
I don't recognise right from wrong
I can't tell every lie from the truth
I trust too much and too slow

I guess, I guess, I'll guess no more
I don't want your fidelity
And we'll kiss, and we'll kiss, and miss no more
Just give me honesty

When we talk I want a break from that
I really just want the real you
I won't settle for a fantasy
And sure It'll hurt and I'll burn
Just like any other man out there

But I want the reality

I guess, I guess, I'll guess no more
I don't want your fidelity
And we'll kiss, and we'll kiss, and miss no more
Just give me honesty

So feed the fantasy in your ego's mirror
You tell me what you think I'll like
You tell me that you are there
Maybe, and perhaps I believe you
So why do I still feel so lonely
Like a relationship made out of air?

You're romancing my heart
I tell you you're romancing a stone
If you're romancing my heart
I tell you that I am still alone

Bruce Gorton

A Woman of Today

My mum used say, "Do you think you're a man?":
Because I go to M&S and BHS,
Debenhams and John Lewis—
To shop in the menswear, no less.

I buy jumpers, casual shirts and long-sleeved tops,
Rugby shirts, cords, chinos and trousers,
I only really buy women's jeans,
And now go to Primark, where I'm a browser.

I'm not a lesbian or a bisexual,
I don't have the sexual to reason,
That my scientific, male orientation,
Is not a case of insanity or high treason.

I did a joint degree,
In Computing Science and Management Studies,
Not flowery English or feeling Theology,
Where you describe social norms and modalities.

A geek I am, from when I was seven—
And a geek is a geek forever;
My computer is my thinking sanctuary,
In which I feel free and clever.

My mum may simply be a fundamentalist Christian,
But she is with many others who get angry,
At cross-dressing, frivolous and effective,
Done with no apprehension or charity.

They've got to accept today's society,
Techno-spurred and women-powered,
We communicate without physical image,
By texts and emails sexlessly rendered.

Women used to lack 'the male voice'—
On the podium of masculinity and employability;
But now we are just part of the workforce,
Not the Land Army or engineers for hostilities.

Although we will always be in the minority—
As women who wear men's clothes,
Our right to do so is today unquestioned,
Because we are not slowed by traditional woes.

I respect Sheryl Sandberg, former COO of Facebook—
A manager, computer scientist and game-player;
And hope that other women are similarly empowered,
To haemorrhage sexism's venomous layers.

More women should go into computing,
Which celebrates diversity, possibility and actuality;
That we are arts oriented and socially aware,
Is repugnant to me and my curiosity.

Computing uses algorithms by logic and truth,
In programs with a set language to enable,
Recursion, functions and procedures,
Specifying user actions, each with individual fables.

When I was thirteen I used to fear,
That I would be mistaken as strange or insane,
But now my fashion is considered just as cool,
As Kate Moss's catwalk, the trending lane.

My modality is my identity:
Without it I am hurt;
So I hope that you can accept my homage,
To modern times in which I have some purport.

Dominique Green

Part Seven

Awe, Wonder and our World

Keeping on the same general landscape as the previous section, when a humanist looks at the world around them, looks at the universe surrounding them, there are often feelings of awe and wonder. But we do not feel we owe such awe and wonder to a god. We marvel, sure. Sometimes we are incredulous. But we don't throw our hands up and say, "Wow, isn't God amazing! He's the only explanation for such beauty and complexity!" No, we strive to be more intellectually open and rigorous.

Beauty is indeed a hot topic for philosophers. It is my opinion, however, that there is more to marvel at with the idea that forces of nature and reality in front of us are responsible for such beauty, shape, complexity and spectacle. This is similar to notions of meaning in life. To me, it is far nobler to create my own meaning derived from that around me, using my critical faculties, than to accept unquestioningly the meaning that a superdeity has enforced upon me.

The same with beauty and the universe around us. There is something worth dwelling on in that notion that we don't need for a god to cause and define that universe—that beauty, that spectacle—when we are appreciating it. Whether it be an incredibly complex yet symmetrical mathematical equation, a butterfly's wings or the expansive Hubble space telescope pictures of nebulae and clouds of space dust and gases, there is much to marvel at in the universe. It's even more marvelous that there is no painter at nature's easel.

Earth's Language

The prairie seas of grass
That carried me on the song
Of the dancing scissor tail
As it mocks and flicks upon the wind
That it dares climb

Its feathers shine brilliant
A rush of sudden orange
A beak turned forward
It catches prey
Of the hopping kind
Of the scurrying kind
Of the flying kind

A journey called earth we are on
We need not embark on religious reasonings
To understand the deeper drifts of time
As sand builds castles on the wall
It carves them out of limestone
and granite is the sculptor of plenty
The deep ocean currents
The winds of season
The leaves of oxygen
The mountains of water
The forests of fruit
The animals of ancestors

We are one as we breathe as one
Our breath is mine and mine is yours

We do not connect because we must
We breathe because we are
Shimmering ice
Will you smile upon me?
It weeps in the sun
Feeding the trout
And the trout become one with the trees
And the trees are my brothers and sisters
Like they are my kin

I can build my house with the mighty pine
I can canoe into the heart of the forest
And listen to the chime of many birds
Or the harrowing of the wolf
Why is that not reason enough?

Why must churches be built as if in defiance against the land?
Quantity over quality?
But this I tell you
It does not matter if god exists or not
Earth will always thrive
The moon will shine as it always has
With or without our presence
The best we can do is appreciate the purest rhythm of nature
Violent as she can be and even unforgiving
She is also my calling
Far more than a bible could ever be

Kristi Hendricks

The Confidence of Camellias

Most of what God or Nature has made
is Nothing
in the dark, vast expanse of Space
billions of miles of Nothing—
not even air
with its oxygen and hydrogen,
its formation of fat rain clouds
or blazing tornadoes
or warm winds
blowing through every tree and beaver,
every ladybug and mother,
every ocean and fog
in every village and time
on this very precious,
Rare Green Dot
that does not even begin to understand Nothing.

Note now
a pale yellow and milk-colored Camellia
basking in the hot sun
enjoying the refreshment of a breeze
and the very noisy visit of a fat, black bumble bee.
What did this Camellia do
to deserve such an Appearance
such Delicate Softness
such Color
such Dainty Respiration
such Aroma
such Robust Life
in the huge reality of
this Endless Blankness of Nothing?
Or is her life
not just her Will
but first Nature

first one of the most Colorful Gifts
in the middle
of so Very Much of Nothing?

And if this singular Camellia basking in the Sun
is so rare
in this Vast Expanse of Blackness
then how rare
are You?
Or, tell me,
are there more of You?

If the very Soul of Nature
is alive and operating in
the Color and Respiration and Aroma
of this one unthoughtful flower
in a blank Universe
then, I wonder,
what does this Fraction of Holiness have to say?
Indeed, if the very Soul of God
is alive and operating in
the Color and Respiration and Aroma
of this one You
in a blank Universe
then, I wonder, what
does this Fraction of God have to say?

Or am I in a hurry
afraid to stop—
considering myself 100% worthless if I actually stop—
defined only by What I Have Done
what I will do today
what I will do tomorrow—
certainly not by any nuanced look
at Who I Am
that Huge Detail of Who You Are

that humor, or intelligence, or kindness that is you
that endlessly without effort
reaches for the sun
defining what Nature has grown
more Complex than Camellias
what God has made
much Deeper than Air.
You sitting there smack dab in the middle
of So Very Much of Nothing
like the Camellia
made Endlessly Beautiful
long before
you ever did anything.

A singular milk-colored Camellia
in a Huge Black Universe
so subtle in color
crisp in shape
so smelly
so ebullient,
while so very unable to think
or see
as you do.

So who are you
standing there Red-Cheeked
Curly-Haired
Mad as a Hatter
or Peaceful as a Camellia
trodden-down or Proud as a Peacock
here for such a brief moment
pondering these cool breezes on your naked shoulders
this hot sunlight on your face
this Day of All Days—
but rare Nature exposed,

a Colorful Aspect of God himself revealed
Fate falling through Black Holes
a Gift of Holy Moments,
as Unthoughtful Camellias
and Ebullient Sunbathers
always are.

C. W. Barrett
Pt. Reyes Station, CA (2008)

See Me Like you Do Her

celebrate woman—
we come from her
mountain moon belly:
(perhaps she brings
one pretty bug
to a blue diamond forest place)
listen—
she cries once;
urge, moan,
sacrifice the silent moment
then her legs part
and a small warm
Universe
is born.

Maureen O'Keefe

Simon

I am Simon who walks between your conscience and your animal self.

You met me the first time you took a step on the earth, spoke a word and looked up at the stars in the night.

I was with you when you learned of fire, found shelter in a cave, and expressed an idea with a symbol.

I gave you Art, beauty and love and freed you from ignorance and fear, only to be slain many times by those who will not know themselves.

But I shall never die! For the forces that gave me life are very strong.

I am the fetus that resides in the womb of your mind.

You, my mother, will some day give me birth, and I will claim my rightful place in the universe.

When conscience is more powerful than animal instincts, the human soul will be born.

Rich Goscicki

The Great Unknown

All that we know about everything
is a fraction of what we don't know,
we're trying to find where we came from
but we haven't a clue where we go.

We're alive on a planet in space
and we try to survive if we can,
but all we know for certain is
we're a species of human called man.

On the whole we're not doing too bad
destroying the planet at will,
with those who believe we can live in peace
sent into war to kill.

To be sure there is a future
not just for the human race,
Surely we should respect our planet
and the hazards it faces in space.

Take a look at the wonderful universe
such a picture of beauty and grace,
and everything that goes on out there
helps to keep our world in its place.

Norman Littleford

What strange creatures

What strange creatures we are
How we fill up our time
And foster our fear
And run ourselves ragged
And fall to our knees
In a powerless fold

What strange actions we take
When we disagree
When we cannot know
But just.
Disagree
Those strange moments of murder
Brought on by a desperate resolve

What strange power we have
To exterminate the past
To annihilate the evidence of
Alternative belief
To desecrate and damage
To vandalise and crush
The testaments of time

What strange lack of wonder
What strange lack of awe
At the infinite stretch of space
At the infinite list of life
What strange lack of wonder
At the beauty in the stars

What a strange, raging blindness to the splendour of life

Gareth Howells

Old Wonders

I must be left without any divine right
For my greatness is subtle in this time
My ideas are new to me, thinking myself
That every rumination has been somewhere at sometime
Burrowed maybe, or perhaps blossomed I hope
But as I pursue my (average) day
They come without a trace from their lineage
Changing no essence, but drifting to a new carrier

Hunter Kettering

Life

A game with no rules
Except physics
A novel without any plot
Unplanned, without meaning
Just patterns
Despite that,
It's all that we've got

Mitchell Cole Bender

Home

Where will we go
when we have no home.

Stuck on this ball
cold and alone.

We truly knew better
but refused to act.

Not from the knowledge
but action we lacked.

"Too late" we all said
without even trying.

So we sat and we watched
as our planet lay dying.

Jaynee Haygood

Picasso Series

Where the songbirds
once went in winter,
warm rains dripped
from jungle leaves.

Ebony and mahogany
spread their welcome
until rumors of industry
reached the riverbanks
and cultivation
crept closer to the mountains.

Some say it doesn't matter
whether life abstracts itself,
a detail at a time,
like a Picasso series,
until nothing is left
except pure electricity.

They could be right.
Light is clean and simple,
but I will miss songbirds.

Linda Armstrong

Stardust

Gaze at the night sky
See the blanket of stars
Expanding through space and time
Suddenly you can't breathe
And you wonder why you're alive
And who you were created by
The answer stares back at you
Though you don't realize

We are all stardust
Science has shown us
We are all stardust

Mysterious and beautiful
Violent and cruel
It's amazing how the universe
Is so much like you
When it's time for stars to die
They explode across the sky
And you would not exist
If it was not for this

We are all stardust
Truth is within us
We are all stardust

The stars died for you

Steve & Tally Cass

Well Seasoned

Amazing, the complexity and dung;
Soaring fliers wing my heart away
While molds and grubs steady my feet
Upon the fruitful, ever-changing earth.
New blossoms' leafy beards fan the breeze,
Reach for space between ground and stars,
Promising abundance once again.
Oven-baking in Summer's sun,
Discomfort is banished by remembrance
Of how I longed for this in Winter.
Wet upon the tongue, slicking eyebrows,
Blurring views, rain is a drink for
The skin of my body, puddles to play in
For the child that remains in me—
Rainbows to hold my breath.
Sodden footfalls trail the leaves
Along the path to seasons' end:
The hermit in my head paces
Gratefully into hibernation.

Christopher G. Doyle

Our Small Space

We live in a place called the present
between yesterday and tomorrow,
the space stays the same but the time running through it
we can neither regain or borrow.

This is what we call our world
all our knowledge is based on the past,
this space will remain here forever
but I wonder how long we will last.

We have tried breaking through the barriers
to look into the future somehow,
but it seems that all we can do is wait
until the future becomes the now.

There are many different societies
each with their own set of laws,
but too many think the others are wrong
and this too often leads to wars.

There is everything here that we need
if we use it the best way we can,
after all we are not alone in this world
we are just one small species called man.

Norman Littleford

What Gift Reveals All?

The morning rises cool
still wet from showers
a wandering breeze teases
jerky shivers upon my nakedness
the scent of soapy lavender in my nostrils
now within the Largest of Skies
Ancient Airs
Fates
through windows air open
unbridled
until, wait, there's a knock
or nudge
on my psyche
my spiritual door
opens
meeting the same Air
Nature
Force
that spoke to John Muir
each of his New Mornings in Yellowstone
or to Lewis and Clark
in each brand new breath of Montana sky
so cold, so large
so full of hope.

That same Air, God
New Day
that spoke to the full
or needy hearts
of Johnny Cash and Umm Kulthum
as they chanted their way
our way
through the barbs of life.

177

That same fresh, New Morning
that spoke to Walt Kelly and Pogo
when they were here,
that spoke to Chagall
as he too penned his colors
the same impetus, passion
churning inside Gandhi
Elizabeth Stanton
our Martin Luthers or Harvey Milk
as they suffered
invented
challenged us forward.

Indeed, that same morning Breeze
or God
or New Day
who awoke Einstein
to his daily math in Switzerland
or John Lennon to tunes playing
in his head
or on a gut string guitar in Liverpool
or to the songs
passions, people
hopes
thumping now large in my chest
sprinting me ever forward
my tender head now steeped in devotion
thankful
for this Generous Morning
here—
by all means here—
for this Moment
so full of so many
now gone,
unlike so many others
now departed.

Yes, my family
is the Family of Us
all of us
this human survival
from when we barely began
to now
with the help
of every creature God has made
every bird and fish
bison and beaver
who brought me forward
every redwood and pine
each Yugoslav and Vietnamese
Buddhist and Catholic
child and grandma
rich and poor
each man and woman
even the dead
some now gone so long
each bearing blessings
many too large to measure
many
too long to count
so full of so many
now gone,
unlike so many others
now departed
I now the recipient
of everything
Nature has spoken.

Indeed, how invested
how pregnant
is this Ancient Morning
Breeze

God or Fate
who awoke me to my own revelations
creations
these original Melodies
the Songs of this Day
which do now reveal
anew
everything
Nature has spoken.

C. W. Barrett
Nehalem, OR; 2015

The Universe Came From Nothing

Stephen Hawking says that the universe came from nothing,
And uses M-theory to deliberate upon the original scene;
Whereas before thinkers saw small particles as the first life,
Now miniature strings beam in a microwave background clean.

Some theorists posit that many universes came and collisions
Occurred until an equilibrium settled when order took the stand;
Observation dictates that the universe must have expanded,
Over time to make the planets that today we all understand.

A singularity must have existed, most definitely,
Some say, if you travel back in time long enough,
With nothing as its identity and composition,
If nothing can be called in any way a description.

Lawrence Krauss argues that nothing can't be defined,
That it's like saying that the universe came from "a potentiality",
'Cos linguistics of any kind require that something exists:
I exist precedes my view that nothing existed, in actuality.

In searching for the initial terms of life,
We must be asking to define negative logic, logic's inverse;
Rational thought drives our cosmological frameworks and states,
And so its inception must be inversely structured, converse.

Believing in god presupposes a reason for his existence,
That is, if we stay within our logic and rational minds;
But without the mind what have we got?
A meaninglessness and an illness that make us truth blind.

And please remember, that the mind is physical, essentially:
Psychology and hurt are made of neurons, hormones;
It is the case that all things can be physically decomposed,

181

And it's philosophical ontology's quest, its great description proposed.

The Big Bang may or may not have occurred, maybe,
But I think we came from nothing in the beginning;
I'm proud to say that life gave me something from nothing,
Chuffed to say it gave me something for nothing for free!

Dominique Green

[Ancient fragments of grace]

Ancient fragments of grace
alien and comatose,
silent-knowers as the Gods
who breathe the air of a world
strange to them.
Atop peaks of celestial mansions
they are still waiting
lost.

And the sea has growled
before the great cities.
So it roars now
and will
indifferent
when we are all gone.

Roy Liran

1P/Halley

Past distant stars my remnants trail
With vapors spread, I loft my tail;
Of ice and stone my body formed
By vacuum chilled and starlight warmed
I see you try; I watch you fail.

Across the starlit sky I tread
As soft I go above your head,
Before you were, before you knew
My form across the heavens flew,
And will fly, still, when you are dead.

Unwatched, I saw new creatures roam,
I welcomed Caesars to their throne,
And when again I passed them by
And cast a glimpse with flick'ring eye,
Do none remain? But more will come.

I saw from distance gods revealed,
Saw prophets called and kingdoms sealed,
And gods destroyed while peoples weep.
(Those gods now in the heavens sleep,)
But gods grow from a fertile field.

Oh Man, whose short stay brings such pain
I pass you by, but still remain
To orbit and observe your strife,
The follies of your tiny life,
From high atop the heavens' plain.

Believe you not that meaning found
Is permanent, and wings around
While fleeting life you wile away
In dark of night and warmth of day,
Your final meaning's in the ground.

Fight not for wealth; I know of gold,
Have seen its luster, far less bold
Than simple clouds that pass me by.
For this, love fails and children die?
Its warmth is false, its glimmer cold.

What do your prayers seek? Is it just?
True piety, or simply lust—
For life continued, death on hold?
Eternal mind, but body cold?
Show me what faith avails for dust.

You want for love; would power suit?
For kindness crushed with cruelty's boot?
When taking that which should be given,
Creating hell where should be heaven,
The sweetness lost; 'tis bitter fruit.

Oh, strive ye not; for naught you'll find,
Exhaust ye not, but fill your mind,
Lest emptied out your life expire
Match-sticks for the funeral pyre,
Bereft the joy lost to your grind.

Live my example and be free,
Asail along our galaxy;
I wrong no man, I fear no wrong,
But drift above and write my song,
In debt to none but gravity.

'Tis true, I am a senseless rock,
But soon you will run out your clock,
Pick out your farm and sign the lease,
Thus perish, decompose, and cease.
Whose weakness then shall Nature mock?

Renounce your claims upon the Earth,
Recall your life before your birth.
Our fate is one, for all that is
Embrace your brother, yours is his!
Oh, recognize your common worth!

William Gunn

Everyday Enchantment

I believe that virtue consists of something more than mere belief
And that just crossing my fingers won't bring health or relief
Shouldn't love be based on virtue, not on ancient ways
And am I to think that this was all created in only seven days?
Looking at the sky makes me feel amazed, confused and tiny
But due to wonders quite different, both dark and shiny
I have my ways to study, to mend this sweet confusion
Rather than talk of mysterious ways with no real conclusion
Why limit your opportunities because of what a sky ghost said?
Do you deny healthy things because of people long dead?
You say my life is empty because I took time to find my road
I would rather earn it than just accept what your book showed
There are plenty of things mysterious here, from a cell to a star
If you seek comfort in illusions, you have gone too far
Consider the following if it is miracles that you crave
It's against odds too high to comprehend that you're here with us
today

John Hawksworth

The Flame in Floyd's Eyes
(a Meditation on The Light)

A Fire burning
snapping boldly
wood being eaten alive
by the heat
hot
bright-orange chunks of burning embers
warming my cold bones
my frost-bitten hands
even my cold toes enclosed in thick wool socks
this Fire now heating my entire home
my entire life
that same exact Fire that burns
the size of our Sun
the daily source of heat for every living Lizard
each lumpy Cabbage and Potato
every one of my Tears, Bright Ideas, Mistakes
this Light the daily source of lip-smacking food for
every fat Bison and Duck
my plump self
in every season
the heated source of each puffy-white Cloud
every gushing River and Rain
each churning Ocean and Tide
this Fire
the creator of the very crust we walk upon
the very Stage on which our dramas unfold
even burning beneath your feet
so molten and hot there right now
a raging Fire
two miles below your cold toes
or spouting thick, hot bubbles
and spurts

in Yellowstone
for only the sixth billionth year
since that Light first shone on us.

This hot, Life-Warming Fire
this Illuminating Light
our only source of the visible
gradually lighting all my mornings
adding color to all those lost gray shapes
showing me all of the Greens in my now tall forest
a new pink glee in my aging face
the subtle, muted Blues in my now large sky
revealing every talent and aspect buried in Nature
yellow-blossoming cactus in summer
white crusty snow in winter
the fluorescent turquoise Light shining through
the surf now falling
a Larger Truth lit here
revealing every talent and aspect buried
in me as Nature
in you as Heat
that angry frown, that proud house built, that sweet song
rendered
Your Larger Truth available, lit here in this Moment
this same Light now cast upon the moon
even as I sleep
this same Sunshine
eventually waking every living thing
the creator of every one of your days since time began
propelling my hot toast & berry jam
my sweaty work, those warm wet kisses
under its generous spell
as it has done daily for 350 million years
for every Gopher and Redwood and Ladybug
our only source of hot life
touching, warming, showing me the way

the author of my Fire Inside
98.6 degrees hot
every hour of every one of my days and nights since I first
arrived
while my teeth chatter outside.
Yes, without this Warmth was not anything made that was made;
and without this Light
you couldn't see any of it anyway.

How does so much Warmth happen
for so long
offering so much to so many?
And how does something so big
(1.2 million earths would fit inside our Sun)
talk so delicately to something so small
as Rabbits and Redwoods
Me and You
Us and Them?
Touching something so rare
as one small, singular planet spinning
warming, shaping, nurturing
something as small as two Blades of Grass
poking-out of hard rock
warming, shaping, nurturing
each witty Intelligence, bellowing Opera, plate of hot Spaghetti
a patch of cold Moss deep in the Woods
hot new Babies in blankets
this Heat the source
of each nail pounded
every kindness or rant raved
each hot cheek enjoyed
every memory playing here so clear
the Light in Floyd's eyes
the Ebullient Spirit in each Creation
the Warmth of your Hot skin
the very Soul of Man

the source of each pounding Passion
wet Despair
buoyant Hope
this warm unassuming blessing
this Hot Gift given
burning brightly in every sky
snapping now in my fireplace hot
melting hard rock even as I speak
these breathed words brought to you by
every hot beat of that same Fire
pounding now
in my Large Heart.

C. W. Barrett
Inverness, CA (2006)

Part Eight

The Bible

As holy books go, the Bible is the big one. It's the bestseller (literally) that's had everybody talking for, well, a few thousand years. God used to get involved quite a bit. There was a feverish number of interventions, meddling and micromanagement. And yet it does seem odd that God has been on a two thousand year holiday. And he didn't take his mobile phone. That said, the world's got on just fine without him. Yes, we have troubles, but much of this comes down to our proclivity to live too closely with each other, and to reproduce too much, and to do things to excesses. We'll work it out, I hope.

But I would rather be living now than in a time when God codified and countenanced slavery, the stoning of adulterers, apostates, people who picked up sticks on a Sabbath and any number of other outdated moral absolutes. The Piraha tribe are one of the few atheistic tribes in history, and they get on just fine without a holy book. Just fine. In fact, so well that a Christian missionary spent thirty years trying to convert them before finally deconverting himself!

The Bible is a confusing amalgam of genres, authors, places and agendas. A simplistic reading of such an array is very difficult. In fact, quite often, literalists do not do it justice. The beauty and power can be seen in the allegorical excellence in some of the claims, not in a simple understanding of literal and historical truth.

As a tool for revelation, some might say that it is a prime example of divine miscommunication. When things aren't clear, it is difficult not to conclude that miscommunication has taken place.

When you add into the mix that this would have been predicted and has been allowed to maintain, then we get an difficult predicament for the believer. There are some 42,000 different denominations of Christianity. There is something for everyone! If you hate gays, if you love gays, if you hate slavery, if you love slavery, if you hate rich people, if you love money…and so on. It is terribly easy to cherry pick the Bible. And given that it was used to countenance slavery for so long, and God would have known this was to happen, we have a problematic method of revelation.

All of which provides rich and fertile ground for atheistic poetry, no?

Telephone Game

From thought, to language,
To sound waves, to brain waves,
Full circle to thought

So many translations
In communication:
So many occasions
For loss and mutation

Mitchell Cole Bender

The Temple

Throats were the fountains of that edifice,
Jetting crimson, steaming in hot air,
Blood-smell and open-gut-smell
Warring with incense, and winning;
Busy butcher-priests labouring red to the shoulders
Under shrieks of animal panic.
Sheep, oxen, goats, doves, by dozens daily,
By hundreds on holy days—fortunate beasts,
To die in such a cause, and such a temple.
Their deaths, one would hope, gratified God;
A bit of a waste otherwise, such a lot of pain
And terror, and nothing to show for it
But bloody flagstones and some very full drains.

Rebecca Bradley

Free to Err

The secrets of the bible are sealed,
out of God's love for men.
truths and enigmatic mystery,
tucked 'tween the pages within.

A simple person like me is not fit to interpret
or even understand,
—the good lord wants it so—suffering is right and just,
recall the fall and God's curse on man.

I'm not wise enough to know all truth,
don't pretend to understand,
but if Jesus paid the price, why then the collection plate
passed 'round Sunday to pay a preacher man?

Simple believers are never worthy,
to explain God's holy word
they'll tell you so, in a pious squint,
at least that's so inside the church;

the service ends and the brethren leave,
heading separate ways,
bound to cross an unbeliever, they're transformed,
giving expert witness by power of almighty grace:

"Believe in the Holy Ghost
and the only begotten Son,
through Jesus Christ ye shall be saved,
by the power of his sacred blood.

"Spare yourself from His infinite wrath
that shall fall as lightning on the unbeliever,
Just believe in the Bible as His inspired word,
faith alone in the blood of the redeemer.

"Darwin may claim man came from ape,
but the truth is within this Holy book,
God formed man from the dust of the ground,
you must only take a look!

"Read here for yourself, the book of Genesis,
oh how Darwin lied, kind begats kind!
—created them male and female—,
commanding, 'Be fruitful, Multiply'."

What is this? You who know all truth?
from times and places you have never been,
of things you have not seen,
nor having any evidence?!
This book you call Holy, Sacred, Inspired, Truth,
claiming divine origin for its creation,
yet, I find your faith rather crude.

That book holds all secrets,
even the origins of life itself?
If life was formed from "simple dust",
then why hasn't science discovered this yet?

You say science cannot be trusted,
and Darwin told a lie, you say man
and ape are un-related,
yet, look what I'm beholding with my eyes:

Wasn't it you sitting in yonder church,
with open mind to what preacher says "just believe",
as they say, "monkey see monkey do",
aren't you remarkably good at mimicking!

You tell me here, that science books,
Darwin, Evolution, cannot be trusted by men,

yet 40,000 denominations,
all EVOLVED from one Christianity!

You say the Bible need not explain
the geological record or modern astronomy,
neither is there mention of chromosomes or telomeres,
the microscopic fabric of DNA.

If the Bible fails to render all truths,
why should I render my faith?
if your God and Bible are free to err,
then so am I, what to say?

Sharon Mooney

Tree of Life

A Tree of Life
They called it,
Never mind
It was written
On animals' skins

A Tree of Life
They called it
As one by one
Its leaves
All withered and died

While all along
Our tree of knowledge grew

A Tree of Life
Some call it still:
That desiccated husk
Of ancient ideas

Mitchell Cole Bender

Genesis 4

I was conceived with joy but was born in pain
And I am Roy I am and I am slave.
I have wronged as I have done well
And done well as wronged
And in success, I found no success.

My countenance has fallen and I knew not why.

I said unto me—if I do well or if I do not do well,
Sin lies at the door and unto me is his desire
And I do not always rule over him.

I said to myself.

And one day in the field I rose against myself.
But how I disappeared I knew not
For I am not my keeper.

But my voice cried to me from the ground.
And in truth—my sin is too great to bear. I am damned.
Now I am a fugitive and a vagabond upon the Earth.

Upon my brow I have set a mark
So that all who find me my shall find me unseen.

                                        Roy Liran

Per Ardua Ad Astra
(Through Adversity [or Struggle] to the Stars)

A fellow by the name of Elijah
Said, "Lord, I'd be pleased to oblijah
By joining your fight
And cheerfully smite
Anyone who dares to derijah."

God said, "Take a month's trial, Elijah,
And I'll let you know when I've trijah."
Then after a week,
Said, "I thought you were meek,
But your bloodlust has sure fortifijah!"

Elisha asked, "When will you rijah
Steeds into the sky, dear Elijah?
You've taught them to fly,
Out of town on the sly—
I know cuz last week I spijah!"

"Be quiet, I don't want to chijah,
But I can't go up yet, said Elijah;
First I must slay
'Bout a hundred a day,
So keep it a secret insijah."

He slew so well, God said, "Elijah,-
For your services I'm going to guijah
To join me in heaven;
Please come about seven
In this chariot that I have supplijah."

Stan Trent

199

Genesis 20/26

Abimelech lusted
after Sarah's lithesome
Syrian limbs...

...or was it lovely
Rebekah's, a few pages on?

Never mind, it's a
fornicating good story,
worth being recycled
in such a good book.

Rebecca Bradley

Eve's Secret Song

After the heavens
and earth had been
sorted out,
after God's Garden
and his Man,
he made me,
the end
of all Creation,
not its after-thought,
but its reason:
I am the rib
and time
is in my side.

Linda Armstrong

Second Time Around

Two thousand years later...
   Christ came back.
But this time to New York.
He got arrested for panhandling
And preaching without a license.
After he got out of jail,
He spoke to the world on TV
Using a free-speech minute.
He told us we had it all wrong.
All the churches,
All the congregations,
All the prayer meetings,
All the bible studies.

  All wrong.

  So....

We crucified him again.

      Christopher G. Doyle

Ecclesiastes

I saw under the sun the place of judgement, wickedness,
righteousness and iniquity was there.
Surely oppression make a wise man mad
For who can make that straight which he hath made crooked
I turned myself to behold wisdom
The fool foldeth his hands together
Better is a poor and wise child, who hath not seen the evil work
that is done under the sun.
The excellency of knowledge is that wisdom giveth life to those
who have it
There is nothing better than that a man should rejoice of his own
works
I turned myself to behold wisdom
The fool foldeth his hands together

Allison Reed

FIG-GET-ME-NOT!

While out walking with his gang,
Jesus felt a hunger pang.
At last a fig tree he espied—
"Now we'll have a feast", he cried,
"I'll stuff myself, and dance a jig!"
But the tree then said, "I don't give a fig!"
And then he saw that it was bare,
No fruit upon it anywhere.
He told the tree, "So that's it, is it?
You're going to regret my visit!"
(Not the words of sycophants—
Prince Charles would not talk thus to plants).
He cursed the tree and struck it dead!
"Now what d'ya think of that?" he said.
Amazing how, with such elation,
he could destroy the Lord's creation.
I think that I will never see,
anyone so treat a tree—
But nothing in this world would boss him;
heaven won't help you if you cross him!
Then, boasting of his latest trick,
this 'perfect man' (and clever dick)
said, "Come on lads; let's make tracks;
looks like we're eating some Big Macs!"

Stan Trent

203

Eve

The bible tells me I was made for and from man
And I must do for him everything that I can
I must surrender to his will, I must submit
I can't make the household decisions 'cause I am unfit
It tells me my place
With ever-lasting grace

The bible tells me I must be silent you can't hear my voice
My role has been divinely defined and I have no other choice
I may not be a teacher of man, I must cover up my shame
These are the laws of the one who in vain I cannot name
He tells me my place
With ever-lasting grace

And my punishment for wanting to learn
Is a painful birth from which I may not return

The bible tells me that I am unclean
I am impure you cannot touch me and it has nothing to do with
where I've been
It is part of who I am, it is because I corrupt man
I was asking for it just by being a woman
He tells me my place
With ever-lasting grace

Shelley Segal

Well, Doom

Well, doom is clearly on the way.
Clouds are gathering,
static charges are
building up at the flashpoints,
and the deluge is predicted
at any moment,
including the next.

But we do not stand idle, oh no!
We are busy laying keels,
carving strakes, building arks, each one
blueprinted by some god or other.

Who wants to hear the nay-sayers
crying in the shipyard,
Your arks are built of stone.

Rebecca Bradley

The Other Bible

Us objects didn't have to believe in anything.
We had no need for passing stories late at night
from one generation to the next.
That's how long we'd lived.

Artifacts excavated in archeological digs
were our ancestors, broken
and catalogued into tiny white boxes.
Our lives used to be so simple.

Now created in seconds on assembly lines,
we've been made to feel like heathen.
We are savages in need of enlightenment.
Factory workers repeat stories that confuse us:

One day their Savior will return,
restoring peace among His Chosen People.
But their true Messiah's already arrived.
His name is Money, and he brings war.

Raymond Luczak

Nahum

If I imagine against the Lord, I will make thy grave
The Lord revengeth, his fury pours out like fire
Who can bide in the fierceness of his anger and still rise up a
second time
All great men were bound in chains, then the chariots raged
All that looked upon the Lord did flee
Behold Lord, I am against thee
Your word is empty and the messages shall no more be heard
Man hath turned away, the Lord dwell in the dust

Allison Reed

Archaeology

The ground defies.
It cannot be seduced
Or broken into rooms.

It will sometime yield, deliberately
Like a trenched soldier.

But the ground does not forget.

Every memory generates deformities
Of color and texture—
Walls.
A shattered jar.
A child's burial.

And like a dead child, the ground
Does not know its name,
Does not bury itself in squares.

It does not cry.

Roy Liran

It Ain't Necessarily So

It ain't necessarily so
It ain't necessarily so
De things dat yo' liable to read in de Bible
It ain't necessarily so

Li'l David was small but oh my
Li'l David was small but oh my
He fought big Goliath who lay down and dieth
Li'l David was small but oh my

Oh Jonah he lived in de whale
Oh Jonah he lived in de whale
For he made his home in dat fish's abdomen
Oh Jonah he lived in de whale

Li'l Moses was found in a stream
Li'l Moses was found in a stream
He floated on water 'til ole Pharaoh's daughter
She fished him she says from that stream

It ain't necessarily so
It ain't necessarily so
Dey tell all you chillun de debble's a villain
But 'taint necessarily so

To get into Hebben don' snap for a sebben
Live clean, don' have no fault
Oh I takes de gospel whenever it's pos'ble
But wid a grain of salt

Methus'lah lived nine hundred years
Methus'lah lived nine hundred years
But who calls dat livin' when no gal'll give in
To no man what's nine hundred years

Jonathan MS Pearce

I'm preachin' dis sermon to show
It ain't nessa, ain't nessa
Ain't nessa, ain't nessa
It ain't necessarily so

George and Ira Gershwin

Part Nine

Free Will and
Other Philosophical Nuggets
(Or, Any Other Business)

In this section I have included a number of poems specifically on free will because it is a subject that fascinates naturalists. In the arguments and debates I have been engaged in, as a philosopher, the free will conundrum is never far from popping up. As well as these single issue poems, there are also, included, some other poems of various philosophical guises.

The following is a poem argument that I had myself with a fellow "Tippling Philosopher" (The Tippling Philosophers are a local pub-based philosophy group from whence I took my blog title "A Tippling Philosopher"). My friend believes in the notion of free will whilst I deny its existence, it being an illusory concept. Guy is a poet, and so his riposte to part of the syllogism I posted was in poetic verse, so I obliged with a further refutation of that:

(1) Every human choice or action is an event.
(2) Every event has its explanatory cause.
(3) Therefore, every human choice or action has its explanatory cause.
Building upon (3), we have our second syllogism:
(3) Every human choice or action has its explanatory cause.
(4) To have explanatory cause is not to be free.
(5) Therefore, human choice or action is not free.

JP's Syllogism- some musings

2) Every event has its explanatory cause

By whose decree?
Do chains only come in circles like the golden chain on your wrist?
The chains that bear anchors aren't circles.
They have a beginning and an end.
They terminate in lonely vacancy,
Where the final link finds it dignity.
They protrude into the freedom of the air,
Colluding with the others.

My poetic riposte

2) Every event has its explanatory cause
A reality Guy, indeed, ignores
By whose decree? He says to me
Why, by observation, common sense and rationality
You see, without causality, science and its method are impotent,
And we must question any scientist's noble intent
To seek the answers as to why things happen (you know, things adhering to laws)
When really Guy is claiming there could be a reasonless 'just because'!

Do chains only come in circles like the golden chain on your wrist? He asks.
Munchausen's Trilemma sets to answer this, that's its task:
It claims things are only grounded in assertion, circle or an infinite regress
But brute assertion makes, of free will, such a mess.

The chains that bear anchors aren't circles, he opines
Without realising that his anchors, if they were accepted (they're not) as fine,

Would only give him brute arbitrary a-rationality
Which is to free will like the moon is to nationality.

They have a beginning and an end, he continues
They terminate in lonely vacancy, okay, so the sinews
Of my furrowed brow continually flex,
I mean, come on, this ain't so complex!

Where the final link finds it dignity, by which he claims
That his anchors magically contain
Rationality, and reasonable grounding
When, as you can see, only brute a-rational floundering
Bases his freely willed decisions, and that's even if
I allow him that brute fact beginning, that abrupt and uncaused cliff
Which starts his causal chain in motion,
But has itself appeared out of a causal vacuum ocean.

They protrude into the freedom of the air,
Colluding with the other, he declares
As if his ruminations make any sense of grounding
Freely willed decisions in reason (for fear of sounding
Like a stuck record, I confess).
Anyway, he's got his work cut out if he seeks to impress.

Jonathan MS Pearce & Guy

To a Naturalist

Beneath, the woods grow dark and deep.
I quake at my imagined leap—
this precipice a life will reap.
Will branches catch me if I fall?
Or will the Underearthlings call?
This bitter bout—a final shout;
my wake and transcendental ball.

In nothingness—in quiet rest
Spinoza's plight I've been bequest—
it leaves me saddened and distressed.
The soul's a comfort in the dark
as losing loved ones leaves a mark.
The end of all—a pitch black wall—
where silence claims the living spark.

The soul's an unclothed human shell.
The pits grow weary—heed the knell;
a sea of blood will serve me well.
I am nothing—bent out of shape;
and silently the gate will scrape
upon a block of greyish rock
where yonder lies the great escape.

Anders Samuelsson

Thoughts about freedom

1.
Machines
Cut the forest
Put it into packets of toothpicks.
Toothpicks!

2.
The trees were here before us
They are not a commodity
The hills were here before us
They are not property
The animals were here before us
They belong to no one
But to themselves.
People were here before us
And people made people into property
And taught us that life is a commodity
And that its goal is profit.

Life is not a commodity
There is no profit without loss.
No property without repression.
No freedom without freedom.

3.
What my hands do—mine.
What my eyes think—mine.
I end where you begin.
You don't belong to me, I don't belong to you.
Let's march together, in one line
And sing about love.

Roy Liran

Reflection (On Free will)

I walked across a gravel path
towards a stagnant pond,
where goldfish swam in circling track,
and stared into Beyond.

Is consciousness a morbid game
to earn ourselves an edge
in gathering up nutrients—
whilst barring sorrows' ledge?

Am I then just a pantomime
of instincts clothed in flesh?
And is love thus an illusion—
the wiring of the mesh?

Bothered by my lonely curse
I quested at the sky:
—"Is truly nothing ever free?
  If so, indeed, am I?"

—"Are we born into illusion
  that tells us minds are free
  and if so can there be ever
  a you, an us or we?"

I shrugged and saw my effigy
breaking instrospection.
I wondered, troubled, what moved first
me or my reflection?

Anders Samuelsson

Identity: who am I to disagree?

That we are not consulted, nor conspire
in human manufacture is a fact
we can't refute. The hidden, forging fire
of persons is a mystery still not cracked.

The further fact of me is doubtlessly
an edifice I embrace; there's little choice
I have but like it. Lumping's not agreed
at all to be an option that you'd voice.

I can't reduce or melt it, slash or burn.
The bomb is off the menu, while camouflage
impossible—to hide me cannot earn
fulfillment's gift or chagrin sabotage.

To accept me, wholeheartedly embrace,
is all that's left, an inconvenient truth.
I'm just a random happenstance in space
I've had to make the most of since my youth.

So, being's nature can't be quibbled, nor
can people argue with existence, say
their accidental atoms they deplore,
allow bare chance by grudge to be outweighed.

My presence, then, a rankling definite itch
that spoils the ointment like a fly, a grain,
alas, which with life's oyster might conflict,
and on its virgin clearness leave a stain.

For grit like me can only irritate,
and cause displacement in the oyster's gloop.
To use another image; an innate
disturbing fox in your serene hencoop.

Propriety won't bear this, it disgusts
idées reçues. The "Managers of Change"
accommodate it poorly for it must
upset, and cause affairs to rearrange.

Alternative to this behaviour might
be suicide, yet who can contemplate
such self slaughter? The famous Dane took fright
and massacred the guardians of the state.

He toyed with immolation, choosing, though,
the bloody-minded option, spiting Claud
and Gertrude, to offend the status quo
and bear the consequences with his sword.

So how can I apologise for things
I didn't guide? When fate prescribed my mien
I was not in on it. Disgrace now clings
with bad names which this feckless dog demean.

Yet, life's the plough to furrow - to avoid
Won't wash at all. The worst scenario
envisaged here is that a person's void,
a meaningless invention here below.

A butterfly might flap its wings and cause
typhoons; a man seeks to equivocate
his entity, set on observing laws
that let him live, but never actuate.

Guy Walker

Temple Cleaning

Some kinds of dirt can't
Be swept under the rug,
Hidden from sight,
Forgotten for good.
To clean, you must look
At the stains before
Attempting to remove them.
It doesn't get done by
Magic, or hopes, or prayer,
Or good intentions.
It requires work
Done willingly,
Though sometimes
Not happily.
Eyes must be opened
To see the view
Through filthy windows
Before you can hope
To scrub them clean.
Airing out the past
Can't be done
Without opening
Doors to the future.

Christopher G. Doyle

[Prescriptures 1:23-24
"[23]For My Kingdom is on the Earth, not that I want it; the
filthy

living body of every man is My dwelling-place, which I do not
clean;

as in heaven or hell, so shall I take up residence within thee on
the

Earth; [24]For thou canst not escape."]

The Supplicant

O mighty soul, which heav'nly vapor wraps,
No rules ensnare, no man-made custom traps,
What Truth, what Light, Thy sulph'rous Pipes contain,
JHVH's harbinger, dread Lord of Gain;

Teach us, thy flock, the way of profits kept,
Of deadlines long forgot, and overslept,
Let not the Stark Fist bash us into shreds,
But keep us safe and lazy in our beds.

No grandeur sought, for none exists to seek,
Our mouths agape, yet feel no urge to speak,
Preferring over prayer our stup'rous drinks,
Excepting "O Bob! Save us from the Pinks!"

To thee, great Bob, our prayer ascends the skies!
To thee, our pittance out the window flies!
For thee, we scorn the wisdom on our shelves!
For thee, we sacrifice our higher selves!

Let not a hard day's work its snares impose,
Let not ambition hinder deep repose;
For none who try advance, though try they might,
And fearful bleating demonstrates their plight.

So when, at last, our mortal clock runs out
Life waxes lifeless; hope recedes to doubt,
When rich men fail to buy a later end,
And paupers into paupers' graves descend,

O then, at last, the Secret is reveal'd
The Great Accounting, leveling the field:
As ODN-1 descends our souls are free—
My Lord, my Bob, accept this Slack from me!

William Gunn

Veal

Immobile
And lonely
I suffer
In silence

For my life
Has a purpose
There's a
Higher power

It's hungry.

Mitchell Cole Bender

I, Pandora

The gods envy your envious nature,
Desire your capricious desires
And lust after a lust such as yours.
They hate the fire of your hatred
And pain to think
How painfully you pain.
The gods fear your fears
And anguish at the thought
Of your eternal anguish.

They know
Sterile gods that they are

That your envy and desire and lust,
Hate and pain—
Make poetry, not prayers.
That your fears and anguish
Will banish them.

For love
I opened the forbidden pythos
To give you these blessings
To set you free.

Hope I kept for me.
For love.

Roy Liran

A Song of Restoration

Shrunken windows, tilted floors.
Broken banisters, lopsided doors
All were once a part of me,
But just look at me now.
All were once a part of me,
now they lie anyhow.

Forgotten kisses, ancient history
My heart is aching, for more
Lost memories, it's a mystery
Who was I before.
Who I am, that's easy
I am just me, nothing more
But who I was, that is teasing me
And I'm no longer sure.

This house has an echo,
As I cross its floor
While it is now sadder,
I've been here before.
And I am now madder,
Of that I am sure.

Sadly dilapidated, Age has touched the house and I
I see my reflection and I wish I could cry
The hairs on my head are now faded and gray
And the echo of laughter has faded away.
So I sit on the stairs,
And I think of the strife
That has ruined this house,
That has taken my life.

Forgotten kisses, ancient history
My heart is aching, for more

Lost memories, it's a mystery
Who was I before.
Who I am, that's easy
I am just me, nothing more
But who I was, that is teasing me
And I'm no longer sure.

And I see in the past,
Through the veil of years
An end to all sorrow,
An end to the tears
Once again in my mind,
The house will stand tall
Restored and renewed,
And that is not all.

Forgotten kisses, ancient history
My heart is aching, for more
Lost memories, it's a mystery
Who was I before.
Who I am, that's easy
I am just me, nothing more
But who I was, that is teasing me
And I'm no longer sure.

As I grasped for the pieces
To build it again
I found I shed the years
And unnecessary pain.
For the house is inside,
It is still part of me
And as I rebuilt it,
It quite restored me.

Who I am, that's easy
I am just me, nothing more

> And I am indisputably
> The child of who I was before.

Carl S. Wagener
(first published on the Church of Virus)

The Vow Of Ahmed El Shalhow

The giant Ahmed el Shalhow
praised the Gods and filed a vow
to shit a sketch of the God Brahma
in thirty years, helped by his llamas,
with runs and normal bowel movement
to achieve karma improvement
into the steppe countryside,
from edge to edge, just two miles wide,
admired from a mesa's top.
The people came and wouldn't stop
to praise the way it was arranged
but suddenly the climate changed
the growing desert was its fate:
a drifting sand dune, seen too late,
now getting closer day by day,
just polished Ahmed's sketch away,
stopped celebrating enthusiasts.
In this life, nothing ever lasts.
It ruined Ahmed's God portrait.
"Now, holy shit", some heard him say.

Alex Dreppec

(sung to the tune of: "God Rest ye Merry Gentlemen")

I'm sorry merry gentlemen, your faith has been mislaid
It isn't true that Jesus Christ was born on Christmas day
The church co-opted solstice to prevent the pagan sway

CHORUS:

It's a crock and it makes me so annoyed
Really annoyed
It's crock and I really get annoyed

And those four gospel 'authors' that you really love to quote
Historians have figured out they're not the ones who wrote
Those contradictory fables based on mirrors and on smoke

CHORUS

And Mary had to be virgin 'cause sex just wouldn't do
You still blame Eve for Adam's fall, your women just get screwed
They say Jesus loved prostitutes, I wonder what he'd do?

CHORUS

Tammuz, Osiris, Mithra, and that's just to name a few,
Each died and then they rose again, had virgin mothers too
Your cobbled-up mythology is really nothing new

CHORUS

Believing that your group is saved, means other folks are not
They're treated all as second-class, no matter what you're taught
You pity them because you think they're going somewhere hot

CHORUS

I've heard your preachers spewing out such bigotry and hate
It seems they only care about a full collection plate
I hope the sheep all wizen up before it's much too late

CHORUS

Chistopher G. Doyle

Afterword

The End of God

Dale McGowan

The end of God was the beginning of poetry and wonder for me. So it's appropriate that this collection begins with God, the thing we must wrestle with, Jacob-like, to get it out of our way.

Then, in the void left by God, the real poetry can be written.

In removing God, we confront the void he was made to fill. There's a genuine existential challenge in being human—a "meaning-rupture," the humanist poet Jennifer Michael Hecht called it, that results from the fact "that we are human, and the universe is not."

It's tempting to pretend that there's no issue there—that the fear of living and dying in a mundane corner of an indifferent universe was made from whole cloth by the religious mind. That's nonsense. If you aren't at least a little disconcerted by our situation, I daresay you haven't thought enough about it. Art can help us engage that reality without illusions, which is why I'm grateful for attempts like this one to express human yearning, love, fear, and wonder with a clear eye and mind.

We've only begun to do it. Imagine what's yet to come.

Dale McGowan
Author, *Raising Freethinkers*

Lightning Source UK Ltd.
Milton Keynes UK
UKOW05f1455091216
289578UK00001B/127/P